Watching My Pa...

DISAPPEAR

Teens Write About
Addiction in the Family

By Youth Communication

Edited by Laura Longhine

True Stories by Teens

Watching My Parents DISAPPEAR

EXECUTIVE EDITORS
Keith Hefner and Laura Longhine

CONTRIBUTING EDITORS
Nora McCarthy, Kendra Hurley, Hope Vanderberg, Sheila Feeney,
Philip Kay, Robin Shulman, and Autumn Spanne

LAYOUT & DESIGN
Efrain Reyes, Jr. and Jeff Faerber

COVER ART
Karolina Zaniesienko

Copyright © 2010 by Youth Communication®

All rights reserved under International and Pan-American
Copyright Conventions. Unless otherwise noted, no part of this
book may be reproduced, stored in a retrieval system, or trans-
mitted in any form or by any means, electronic, mechanical,
photocopying, recording, or otherwise, without express written
permission of the publisher, except for brief quotations or
critical reviews.

For reprint information, please contact Youth Communication.

ISBN 978-1-935552-23-9

Second, Expanded Edition

Printed in the United States of America

Youth Communication®
New York, New York
www.youthcomm.org

Table of Contents

Contents

Using the Book

Introduction

Dealing with a parent who has an addiction can be emotionally overwhelming. It can also be dangerous: Substance-abusing parents often behave unpredictably and have a hard time maintaining a safe and orderly home. Their children are three times more likely to abused and four times more likely to be neglected. In this book, teens write about what it was like to grow up with an addicted parent, and what they did to protect themselves.

Children who live with addicted parents are often burdened with adult responsibilities. These writers describe having to take care of parents and younger siblings, scrounge for their own food, and maintain their households. Many live in fear of losing their parents to an overdose or being separated from them in foster care.

Virtually all of the teens in this book express love for their parents, and yearn to have a close relationship with them. But when parents are not ready or able to seek help and overcome their addictions, teens have to make difficult decisions about how to protect themselves.

In the first story in this book, Chaquana Townsend writes about her conflicted feelings about her mother, who is on and off drugs. Though Chaquana has been placed in foster care, she still desperately wants to develop a close relationship with her mother. But she doesn't know if that's possible. She writes:

"Sometimes I say to myself, 'I refuse to give up on my mother...she's trying to get back on her feet and she needs someone there to support her....Other times, I feel angry at her and want to keep away from her to protect myself from being hurt again and again."

Some writers, like the author of "Making It on My Own," try to cut themselves off from their parents altogether. Other teens, like the writer of "I Think These Drugs Are Daddy's," try to maintain loving relationships with an addicted parent, at great personal cost.

For many, foster care or kinship care (living with relatives) provides a welcome escape from the chaos they experience at home. In the last story in the book, Tamara makes the difficult decision to leave her mother, who has started using drugs again, and move in with her older sister Tasha. "I didn't want to hurt my mother," she writes. "But I felt like staying with Tasha long-term was the only way for me to be in control of all aspects of my life."

When parents are able to get treatment and conquer their addictions, they can re-establish their bond with their children. In "The Man in the Glass," Jessica's alcoholic father is finally able to see the impact his drinking has had on her when he goes to an inpatient rehab center.

In "A Second Chance," Karen Haynesworth is removed from her drug-addicted mother and eventually placed with a supportive older cousin. The cousin gives her a safe and stable home, and also allows Karen to spend time with her mother, who is trying to get clean.

Gradually, Karen and her mother open up to each other and form a bond. Karen is able to express the pain she's been through, and her mother explains how she got into drugs and takes responsibility for the hurt she's caused.

"It was good for me to know who she really is, and to understand why she had such a hard time taking care of me," Karen writes. "I know I am not going to live with my mother again, but I am happy to have a relationship with her."

Interviews expand on how to cope if you're living with an addicted parent, how rehab works, and what it's like to reconnect with a parent who's been through treatment. We hope this book inspires teens in similar situations to seek support. And we hope it reminds them that a parent's addiction is not their responsibility, and it's not their fault.

In the following stories, names have been changed: *I Think These Drugs Are Daddy's*, *Watching My Parents Disappear*, and *Leaving Her Behind*.

Terrence Taylor

House of Cards

By Chaquana Townsend

"No Mommy! Don't do it!"

"I'll kill you!" she screamed.

I was lying on the floor while my mother held a chair in her hand. I felt scared and hurt at the same time. I told her to stop, and she finally put the chair down. She told me to sit on the sofa quietly, and I did as I was told.

As soon as she was out of my sight, I ran outside to get help. I knocked on a neighbor's door. It was the second time I'd turned to her to get away from my mother's abuse.

"Who is it?" she said.

"It's Quani, can I please use your phone?"

She opened the door quickly and let me in. I told her my mother was hitting me again, and she looked at me with pity.

That day I left my mother's house for good. I knew it was for the best, but a part of me wanted to stay.

Ever since I was little, I'd wanted to know my mother. My grandmother raised me from the time I was 4 until I turned 13. All those years I never knew much about my mother. All I did know was that she wasn't capable of taking care of me.

My grandmother cared a lot about me and did the best she could. She provided for me and made sure I was happy. She was the nicest woman and I've never felt a greater love.

Still, I imagined my mother as my knight in shining armor. I believed that if we were reunited, I would be happier. I would feel safe knowing that my mother really cared for me and would always be there no matter what.

As much as my mom has hurt me, I still want that mother and daughter relationship I never had.

My mother would call to check on us. She would ask how we were doing and she wanted to know what we looked like. On the phone I told her I looked fine but I really believed I looked fat, so when my sister would send her pictures I'd tell her I didn't have any. I didn't want my mother to be disappointed in me because of my weight. Her opinion meant the world to me.

My mom also came to visit my sister and me a few times. We'd go to the big fair and the movies. One time my mother only stayed for two days. When she left, my sister and I fell on the ground and cried for hours. Many times we would look at pictures of her, or a card she sent us, and cry. I would throw tantrums because I missed my mother so much.

When I was 13, my grandmother asked my sister and me if we wanted to live with our mother in New York City. We told her yes. Before we left, my grandmother warned me that it wouldn't be a fairy tale. Still, when my sister and I arrived on June 9, 2002, I was ecstatic.

When I walked through the front door of my mother's apartment I fell in love. The furniture was leather and there were knickknacks everywhere. There was a glass mirror in the living room and the floor was a shiny brown. The cabinets were filled with food and food was on the stove. I thought to myself, "This is the life and I couldn't ask for anything else."

New York had so many people and so much going on that my sister and I just couldn't compose ourselves. We went all over the city. We went to 125th St. in Harlem, 149th and Grand Concourse in the Bronx, and so many other places. New York was alive and I loved it. We also went swimming every other day and we went out to eat every week.

I had a good time being a family. What I loved about my mother was her sense of humor. She's really funny! She was always cracking jokes on people.

But living with my mom opened my eyes to many things. I learned my mother was a drug addict. I learned she was dysfunctional and couldn't take care of two teenage girls. I also realized I wasn't ready for the world and I needed somebody to protect me. I wanted her protection, but I couldn't get it.

My mother started using crack again six months after we moved in with her. My sister and I didn't know she had been using crack since the '80s. Everyone in my family knew, including my grandmother, but they never told us. Our mother's addiction was a surprise.

Gradually, my mother's drug addiction got worse and worse, and so did our situation at home. She would sell her welfare check to support her habit and leave my sister and me in the house all alone. She would come in at all hours of the night. There was no food in the house and our money would come up missing.

We grew hate in our hearts for her that we carried around everywhere. Every other week she would say she was done, but it would only last for a few days. We got disappointment after disappointment and it hurt.

My grandmother found out what was going on and sent us

money. We would hide the money in the soles of our shoes, but our mom always found it. My grandmother even came to New York to find a place so we could live with her again, but she passed away five days after she arrived. It hurt me so much. I couldn't understand why God took her away from me. I hated myself for ever disrespecting her or getting smart with her.

After that, my sister and I started going to my father's house and other relatives' houses to escape from my mom.

One day I came home from a family member's house and my mother was home. She was very angry that I had stayed out for two days. She told me I was on punishment and I couldn't go outside. I rolled my eyes and told her, "I'm not staying here." I was very angry with my mother for putting my sister and me through hell. She wasn't ready to take care of us, so why had she said she was?

She told me to fold some clothes. I sucked my teeth in anger but I started

I would like to tell my mom how truly hurt I am by her behavior, but I'm scared she won't understand.

folding. Then she said, "You're going to stop playing with me." She grabbed me by my hair and punched me in the face. I screamed for my cousin to get her off me, and then I left. I was angry and I didn't want to be near her.

The next time she hit me was the last. After she attacked me with that chair and I ran to our neighbor's, my sister and I were taken away from her for good. We were placed in foster care.

After that dreadful day I couldn't look myself in the mirror without thinking of how I hated this woman so much for what she did to me. I was so unhappy. Although I wanted a relationship with her, and I knew I had to forgive her in order to grow some kind of connection, it wasn't easy. I couldn't get past my shock and disappointment at how she'd treated me.

In foster care I started living with my uncle. He told me stories about my mom as a child, like about her stealing money from one of my grandma's friends, or getting upset with my grandmother and smacking her in the face. All the stories were negative. I began to believe my mother wasn't very nice, but I also wondered what about her past had led her to become that way.

We started to go to counseling a few months after we were taken away from her. We had about two sessions together and the rest were only with my sister and me. The two sessions with my mother weren't helpful because she was in denial. She would lie a lot and it only hurt us. So the sessions stopped.

But as much as my mom has hurt me, I still want that mother and daughter relationship I never had. Even though we're not supposed to see our mom, I've continued to see her. I feel like I'm addicted. I can't stay away.

I want and feel I need a healthy relationship with my mother, even though I know I probably can't get it. I fear that without a solid relationship with her I will always be incomplete. I want my mother to be that strong black woman I can look up to.

My mother is an intelligent woman and she knows a lot of people. People are naturally drawn to her. If she would get clean and finish pursuing her education, she would be very powerful. I know she has it in her.

It's been hard to try to build a relationship with my mom. Sometimes I say to myself, "I refuse to give up on my mother because I understand what she's going through. She's trying to get back on her feet and she needs somebody there to support her."

Right now my mother says she's not using drugs, but I'm really not sure if that's true. I try to give her as much support as possible, because she needs it. She's still my mother.

Other times, I feel angry at her and want to keep away from her to protect myself from being hurt again and again. Recently my mother said, "I don't need my kids when I'm not using drugs—I need them when I am using drugs." But we've been there when she's using and she just drives us away. I thought to myself, "When you are using drugs you're uncontrollable."

I think my mother really doesn't know what she wants. She doesn't have the slightest idea about how to be a mother. She doesn't ask us questions and she refuses to open up to us. I guess she's just as scared as I am.

I also feel angry that my mom doesn't know a lot about my past and how her actions affected me. I don't know if I'm ready to tell her, either. We speak on the phone almost every day. She calls me and we go places together, but she's not there emotionally because she doesn't know how. Our conversations are usually short and shallow:

"Hello!"

"What are you doing?"

"Nothing, I'm going to sleep."

"Well, call me in the morning."

"OK, bye."

"I love you Chaquana."

"Uh, I love you too."

I would like to tell my mom how truly hurt I am by her behavior, but I'm scared she won't understand. I want her to know she contributed to my feelings of low self-esteem and that I made foolish decisions because of that. Keeping things from her saves me from her judgment, but holding them in keeps me wondering about her response.

Sometimes when I'm lying in my bed I think about her passing away, and it makes me cry. I love my mother very much. I'm just not sure what to do with my love. I refuse to let her go, but I don't think my mother is putting as much effort into this relationship as she should.

I've started thinking that my strong attachment to my mother isn't going to help me in life. I ask myself, "Why do I make so many excuses for her and why do I feel like I owe her my love?" I've realized hoping and wishing she will change is probably foolish.

With all of these emotions inside of my head, I found a solution I'm going to try. I've decided to set boundaries. I can still talk to my mother, but I have to expect less and give less as we build up trust. I keep my guard up when I speak to her because I know I can be easily sucked in. My emotional side wants to love and care for my mother. My logical side knows I should keep her at a distance to protect myself from possible disappointment. At the end of our conversations now I don't say, "I love you." I say goodbye.

Chaquana was 17 when she wrote this story.
She attended Tuskegee University.

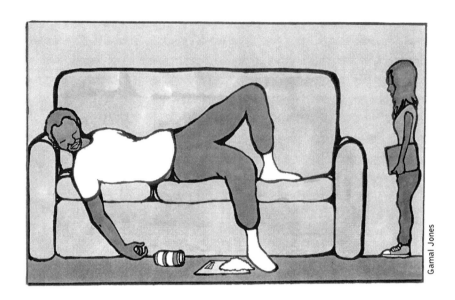

Gamal Jones

I Think These Drugs
Are Daddy's

By Anonymous

When I was 9, my mother told me that she and my father had been crack addicts for about two years, before my two older sisters and I were born. She said smoking crack was very common back in the '80s.

Hearing that my parents had been crackheads came as a surprise to me. The crackheads I saw in my community stank, looked dirty, and begged for money. I couldn't imagine my parents this way. They had an apartment together, they both worked and were always clean. But I felt glad that my mother told me, because it was better than hearing it from someone else.

My mother told me she got off drugs by going to rehab and Narcotics Anonymous and getting support from counselors and family members. She said my dad went his own way, so I figured he used a different method to quit than my mom had. Unfortunately, I soon found out that wasn't what my mom meant.

One afternoon about six months later, my 12-year-old sister came into our bedroom with a small glass bottle, about three inches tall, with a blue cap. There was some type of white powder in it and I was super curious. "Tyleah, where'd you get this from?" I asked.

"Daddy's drawer. You know he does drugs," she said.

I looked at the bottle in amazement. The white powder was drugs! My sister and I played with the bottle for a while, looking at it closely, twirling it around and passing it to each other.

"You really think this belongs to Daddy? Or Mommy?" I asked her. I wanted so badly for it to belong to someone besides my father, even if that person was my mother. It would have been easier to deal with this kind of betrayal from my mom, because I trusted my dad so much.

I knew that if I asked, my dad would tell me the truth. So I didn't ask.

My father had always lived with us and been a big part of my life. He picked me up from school, and often drove the family to Coney Island. Best of all, on nice days, Dad would sit me on his lap and let me steer the car down alleyways and empty streets. That made me feel close to him and like he trusted me as much as I trusted him.

That trust was important to me, because I never felt my mother and I had any trust between us. Everything I told her, whether it was about a boy I liked or problems at school, she'd tell her friends or use against me in arguments. We never saw eye to eye on anything—what I should wear, what sport I should play, or who I should be friends with. I felt she wanted to create me, instead of letting me become my own person. I hated this, so I hid everything from her.

But Dad was different. He'd listen closely to my thoughts, looking into my eyes and nodding his head, trying to understand me. This made me feel important and loved by my father, something a lot of my peers couldn't relate to. Most of them came from single-mom homes and didn't have close bonds with their fathers.

So I was crushed when my sister said, "I think these drugs are Daddy's. He be sleepin' with his eyes almost open and he be havin' that white stuff in his nose all the time." I was shocked. My dad had always told me the white stuff was from eating powdered doughnuts, and I'd believed him.

For a long time after that I didn't let myself think about it. I just hoped my sister was wrong. But when I was 11 or 12 I began to see movies about drugs, like *New Jack City* and *Blow*. I saw characters in those movies nodding off from crack or cocaine, and realized I often saw my dad nodding off that way.

I was scared because those movies always had bad endings like death or jail. I wondered if Daddy would have a bad ending too. I couldn't bring myself to talk to him about it, because I was afraid he'd get upset and because I just didn't want to think about it. So I kept pretending it wasn't happening.

My parents both worked, but I guess my dad wasn't bringing in enough money to support his habit and help out with the bills. I heard my mother and him go back and forth about money all the time.

One night when I was about 13, I was watching TV with my sister, when I heard my parents having another money argument. This one was different, though. It sounded louder and angrier, and for the first time my mom screamed out loud about my dad's drug addiction.

"I'm tired of this, Oscar!" she yelled. "You can't stay here and use drugs anymore. I won't allow my children to be around you this way!"

"Those are my kids too! I do more for you than you would ever do for yourself," my father said.

"Those drugs robbed you of your sense, and even worse, my

best friend. I don't even know who you are anymore. Oscar, you have to leave, for good."

When I heard this I felt hurt. If my father left, what would happen to our bond? I knew he would still come to visit, but things wouldn't be the same. My father came to my room. My sister and I acted like we hadn't heard anything, continuing to stare at the TV. "Kids, I'm leaving. See ya'll later," he said calmly.

"Where you going, Daddy?" I asked.

"For a walk."

Daddy didn't come back for a month. My mom later told me that he'd gone to live in a shelter. I guess he didn't tell me because he knew I'd hate to see him in there.

After that month he started coming to visit us twice a week for an hour or two. My mom acted like he wasn't there, but that never stopped him from asking me how my day was, then telling me to stay and watch TV with him. We didn't talk much, but being with him for those short visits was important to me. For just a little while, it felt like old times again.

One evening about a year later, when I was a freshman in high school, my mom, sister, and I were watching *American Idol* when the phone rang. "Hello?" my mom said. "Yes, this is she. Kings County? For what?"

She got off the phone and told us that my father was in the inten-

Every day I hope he doesn't overdose and die, and sometimes I think only my faith will keep him alive.

sive care unit on a respirator. When I heard I.C.U., I became highly alarmed. I wanted to see him immediately. Although I didn't know why Dad was in the hospital, I somehow knew it had to do with his drug addiction.

"What are we waiting for? Let's go to the hospital!" I said. But my mother told me she wanted to wait a couple of days because she didn't want me to see him that way.

I went to my room and listened to music to try to soothe the thoughts that were now haunting me. I thought my father was going to die. I was scared to see him, but after three days I decided to go there on my own. I wanted to be supportive, like I knew he would be for me.

It was scary. Seeing the machine breathing for him was like watching a scene from a movie. He had tubes down his throat and his chest was going up and down. He woke up when I came in, looked at me with wide eyes and smiled. But I began to cry. He tried to say something but couldn't. He tried and tried until mucus suddenly began coming from his nose.

I got really scared and called out for the nurse. As she walked slowly toward the room, I yelled, "Hurry up, something is wrong with him! What the hell are you walking slow for?"

"Miss, you cannot make all this noise. This is the intensive care unit," she said. I cursed at her and stormed away before she could kick me out. I was frustrated not only with the nurse, but with my dad's condition. Why couldn't he just leave the drugs alone?

A couple of days later when Dad was finally off the respirator and able to speak, he told me he'd been trying to say, "I love you." It made me feel important that despite his condition, he made sure to let me know how much he loved me. Even when he couldn't breathe on his own, he still wanted to reassure me of his love.

My father finally recovered after two months and moved in with his sister in Queens. The doctors said that the drugs had temporarily stopped his breathing. I was hoping this was his wake-up call, but his drug addiction continued.

I still never said anything to him about his drug abuse, though, out of respect and a little bit of fear of what he would say. I didn't want to nag him about using, because I knew that's what everyone else did to him. I thought it would upset him and he might not come over as much and spend time with me. I just wanted him to be peaceful, and I didn't want our relationship to change.

About six months after my dad got discharged from the hospital, I came home from school one day and the house smelled like a homeless person. I walked in to find Daddy on the couch smoking a cigarette. "Hey Larissa!" he called out.

"Hi Daddy." I jumped into his arms and realized the homeless person smell was coming from him. I was worried. What if he was really homeless? I knew that if I asked, he would tell me the truth. So I didn't ask.

"Need some money?" he asked.

"Nope, already got enough," I answered. We sat and talked about a whole bunch of stuff: school, and different jobs that interested us, like being actors and flight attendants. He put his arm around me and the smell got worse. But I acted as if it didn't bother me. Our conversation was more important. Sometimes when he came over he was high and nodding off. But he didn't seem high this time. He sat up straight and paid close attention to our conversation.

My sister has disowned my father, but I remain faithful to him because he has remained faithful and loyal to me.

My dad still visits me every week. He tells me how proud he is of my accomplishments and that he's planning to get his own place in Brooklyn soon and wants me to visit often. But we never talk about his drug use.

Nowadays, Dad looks like the crackheads I see in my community. Every day I hope he doesn't overdose and die, and sometimes I think only my faith will keep him alive.

If I had the heart to talk to my dad about it, I would ask him what his childhood was like, because I believe a person's childhood affects their adult life. I've never heard my dad speak about what happened to him growing up, and I wonder if any of it would give me a clue about why he's addicted to drugs now.

I would also tell my dad that his drug abuse makes me feel neglected and at times like he doesn't care for me. I'd tell him that it enrages me that when he took those drugs and almost died, he didn't think about me or what I would go through if he died. I felt like he didn't care about my feelings or life, only his pleasure.

But while my dad has shown me something I never want to become, he has also shown me what it means to have love and support for someone, no matter what. My sister Tyleah has disowned my father for not being there financially and for not being the kind of father she can talk to her friends about. She claims she doesn't have a father, like he never existed. But to me, disowning a parent would be like disowning your arm, because your parents are a part of you.

Most of all, I remain faithful to my dad because he has remained faithful and loyal to me. Throughout all of his drug use, my dad has always managed to stop by and check up on me. He has always stayed interested in my activities and school. He encourages me to finish school and stay focused. When I think of my dad, I don't think of a drug abuser. I think of how much of a good father he has been to me.

The author was in high school when she wrote this story.
She later graduated and attended college.

Allison Thornton

The Man in the Glass

By Jessica F.

Looking through my family album one thing you will notice is that there's a beer can or a bottle in practically every photo. There's one of my father holding me when I was an infant. In his other hand he's holding a can of beer. In another one, my grandfather is sitting in his favorite chair with a bottle of Bacardi rum by his side. There's one with me and my dad on the ferry boat going to the Statue of Liberty when I was 6. Again there's that familiar can of beer in his hand.

Throughout my childhood my father always put liquor first. He rarely thought about me. I used to like to go to parks and the movies with him, but he was always hanging out with his buddies in the bars. When he did come to see me he always said, "I ain't got no money. I'm broke." I'd look in his wallet and I'd find that he was putting extra money aside for his drinking.

My father rarely treated me with any love at all. He would get aggravated easily and lash out at me. He had no patience for anything and would curse at me and tell me to get out of his face. Once I asked him to come to parents' night and he said, "I don't want to go to that @#$%. Leave me the hell alone."

I tried to talk to him about his problem but he only denied it. I would tell him, "Dad, you're drinking too much. Stop drinking. It's bad for you, you hardly have no money." I would beg him to just try, but he refused.

"Stop nagging," he'd say. "You sound just like your mother." Sometimes I would get so frustrated that I would yell, "Do you want to die like your father?"

My grandfather died from a heart attack when I was very young. I remember seeing him every day in his chair with a bottle of vodka on the table right beside him. Now my father was becoming just like him. He would sit in that same lounge chair in front of the TV, drinking beer. My worst fear was that he would die like his father had and leave me all alone.

I couldn't understand why he did it. He had a job, a home, and a family who cared. He didn't need to drink but I couldn't make him see that. There were times when he would tell me that I was the reason he drank. At night I would cry myself to sleep, desperately wanting to believe it, just so I could know that there was some reason.

After a while I reached the point where I gave up. I stopped fighting with him. I didn't try to talk him out of drinking. I avoided him as much as possible. I just didn't give a damn anymore.

But he only got worse. He'd get up in the morning and grab a bottle of vodka from under his pillow. If he didn't get that first drink his hands would shake so badly he couldn't even hold a cup of coffee. It became too painful to watch.

One time he was drunk on the job and miscounted $1,000. They suspended him for two weeks during the holidays. That year he spent Christmas drinking and sobbing about how he had no money.

Then one night we were sitting in the car and again I was telling him that he was drinking too much. "Shut up!" he screamed. "I don't want to hear it." He put his trembling hands over his ears but I wouldn't stop talking about how he was losing everything: his family, his friends, soon it was going to be his job.

He said he was tired of living this way. He didn't want to live anymore. He wanted to kill himself. Then he collapsed in tears and admitted how his mother and I were the only reason why he lived. "Then tell me why are you killing yourself by drinking?" I asked. "I can't stop," he said. "I'm an alcoholic."

He finally admitted that he was an alcoholic. I knew that was the first step to recovery.

I tried to talk to him about his problem, but he only denied it.

A couple of days later he found out from his union that his job covers treatment for drug and alcohol abuse. He told me he was going away for one month, that he wanted to straighten himself out. The next morning he was gone before I could really say goodbye or good luck.

He went to a treatment center in Pennsylvania. The first four days there he had to go to detox and go cold turkey. That's when you get all the alcohol out of your system and your body is craving for liquor so badly that it hurts. He had to stay in a cabin away from everyone. They do that because the person gets frustrated, angry, and desperate. It must have been horrible for him.

After a week he started to call and tell me how he was doing. At the medical center he learned that he had a swollen liver and a stomach ulcer, and he was treated by a doctor. He said he was going to counseling, support meetings, and physical activity programs. He was eating regularly and learning about his problem.

After two weeks I got a phone call from a counselor asking me to visit the clinic for family week. I was excited about my father's recovery but somehow I didn't believe that he would ever truly stop.

When I arrived I stayed in a house with other close family members of the patients. I discovered that I wasn't the only one suffering. We had sessions where we learned about the things we were unconsciously doing to support the person's habit.

There are times when we mean to do well but instead we provoke the person to drink more. People think if they get rid of the liquor, they get rid of the problem. Wrong! Every time I used to take the beer out of the fridge and pour it down the drain, my father would only go buy more. I wasn't helping him. I was only making him more rebellious. He'd go out and get drunk because he couldn't stand to hear me nag.

At the treatment center I got a chance to tell my father how I felt for the first time. They gave us a piece of paper with incomplete sentences and we had to fill in the blanks: "I never understood why you..." or "It makes me angry when you..."

My father was given the same paper. Then we exchanged papers and sat in a circle and read each other's answers aloud. I found out the one thing that got him upset was when I nagged him. I knew I had just as many faults as he did, but I also knew that it wasn't my fault that he drank.

Then he read my answers aloud. He read how the one thing that I never understood was why he never showed any love toward me. As he kept reading, you could see he was trying really hard to hold back his tears. His voice was trembling and he managed to say he was sorry, that he never realized the pain he caused. Everyone in the room was crying. I didn't think my answers were going to affect anyone but me and him.

Since that day a year ago, my father has changed. He has taken me out on special occasions. We go and visit family for dinner and see movies together. I think my support has helped, but he is really overcoming his alcoholism on his own. He attends his support meetings once a week and visits his alcohol counselor every other week.

Still, each morning he wakes up only to struggle not to have a drink. My father tells me he could easily "relapse" and take a drink at anytime. He did relapse once. Luckily I was there to confront him and help him face himself and his problem. He received treatment and now is recovering again.

This past Father's Day I was so proud of him because it had been almost six months that he remained sober. I gave my father a special gift. It was a poem entitled "The Man in the Glass" to place by his night table. It described how an alcoholic goes his whole life cheating himself out of the truth.

My worst fear was that he would die like his father had and leave me all alone.

I gave it to him to remind him that when he drinks he isn't really fooling anyone else. He's fooling the most important person of all—himself.

When I read the poem it made me wonder how my father could look at himself and live a lie. I pictured his reflection on a glass of liquor, the reflection of a face that told a 1,000 lies all his life. Now that my father is sober, I hope he will never have to face that man in the glass again.

Jessica was 16 when she wrote this story. She went on to graduate from high school and college and became a police officer.

Emily Dinan

Watching My Parents Disappear

By T. M.

"Tracey, get the boys ready for school." I'd overslept and now I was going to be late. My mom lay on the couch. I had to get my brothers ready for school. But that day I decided that my mom and dad needed to be taught some kind of lesson. I ran for the door to escape the small, cramped space that I called home.

It wasn't my plan to tell my teacher about my parents that day. But my parents were using crack, and keeping the secret was hard. I felt like I was watching my parents die. My father was also sexually abusing my sister and me. I felt that if I didn't speak up soon, I would not be able to handle living for much longer.

For many years I had pretended that nothing was wrong, but it was too hard to keep doing that. I was starting to get very depressed. I thought that if I told somebody, my parents would realize they had a problem and that there are people who could help.

In school, I went to my teacher with all of my courage, even though I felt ashamed and scared.

"Tracey, what's the matter?" she said. I sat down thinking maybe this wasn't a good idea. I remembered my mom telling me, "There's nothing wrong with this family. Don't say anything to anyone or you'll be the shame of the family." I tried not to think about what she'd told me.

"My mom and dad are on drugs," I said, almost like it was a joke, but then I started to cry. My teacher was shocked. I said, "Sometimes my parents use drugs so they can feel better." I didn't want to tell her about my dad, because I felt sick, but I did.

My teacher wanted to tell the school social worker, who was my godmother. She told me, "I have to tell. If I don't I could get in big trouble." I didn't want her to, but I said, "OK, you can tell." I felt distant from what I was saying, like I wasn't talking about my own parents.

Later my godmother came over to me. She looked like she'd been crying. She said, "Tracey, is there something you want to tell me?" I told her. She said she

If my parents didn't get their drugs they were violent and would beat us. When they got high they acted like that had never happened.

was going to call Child Protective Services and try to move us out of the house. The rest of the day was even scarier. I was afraid that if my parents found out they would beat me or hate me.

That night, I made dinner, cleaned the dishes, and did my homework. I went to my room and talked to my twin sister. She told me that she was happy that I told.

I wanted to give my mom a kiss goodbye and give my dad a hug. I felt like telling them that somebody was coming to take us all away. I wanted to tell them that I was sorry, but I was too afraid so I went to sleep. That was the day that I changed my life but lost my family.

When I was little, home was the best thing. I loved to run home after school and know that my mom would be there. My dad came home late but we would see him before school in the morning.

Sometimes my mom would turn on the radio and dance with us. She would take my sister and me outside to run around. My dad used to take me to places that sold toys and he would buy my sister and me one each. On Fridays, my family often went for long walks and sang songs together, like "Lamb Chop's Play Along."

But as a child, I also watched my mom go in and out of hospitals for depression. I watched her and my dad argue about the littlest things and fight with each other. And my parents were on crack ever since I can remember. When they took the drugs they made me feel like I was nothing. They treated me and the rest of my family based on their mood. If they didn't get their drugs they were violent and would beat us. When they got high they acted like that had never happened.

Things got worse for all of us when there was a fire and our apartment burned down. We lost everything. My dad left us. My mother and the rest of us moved into a shelter that wasn't always safe. Sometimes our stuff was stolen, and there were gangs around.

All of this made my mom more depressed. Living with my mom's depression made me feel like I was depressed. I wanted to always be depressed like her and to lie next to her and sleep by her all day. I also would try to win her affection by keeping the house as clean as possible and letting her know that I loved her.

I wanted my dad to come and get us, and when he did come back two years later, my brothers and sisters and I were so happy. But everything went from bad to worse. My mom's depression got worse and she got angry. Sometimes she would treat me like

I wasn't there, or she would make me stay away from her.

Watching her change and reject me made me so sad. I felt like I was to blame. And that's when my dad started to sexually abuse my sister and me. At night we would take turns staying awake to protect ourselves, but he would beat us if we didn't do what he wanted.

I dealt with everything by blocking out reality and pretending that everything was OK. As a kid, and even now, I didn't know how to show how I felt. I just wondered how I could make myself feel better. I made myself forget my feelings by eating candy, playing with my toys, and going outside.

My mom would do the same thing. She told stories to cover up her drug use. Once her face was swollen and she said, "Oh, I went outside and a ball hit me." Other times when she'd been using drugs she'd say, "I shouldn't have eaten so much candy!" She made it seem like things were OK, but we knew what was going on.

I was afraid, but I knew that my family wasn't going to get better if nobody did anything about it.

For a while I thought that my mom didn't know what my dad was doing to us. I wanted to tell her, so she would make it stop. But one day I was sitting next to my mom and she said, "If somebody is hurting you, tell me and I'll deal with it." Then I knew that she knew, but she wasn't going to do anything about it.

Then I really hated my mom and I started to feel detached from my parents. I started to think that they would always be two drug addicts. I saw myself growing up in a small jail that had no love and was cold all year around. I stopped loving them and started to blame them.

Finally, I decided to speak up, because I was tired of blocking out reality. When I felt depressed, I couldn't hide from my feelings anymore. I was afraid to face the fact that I didn't really have a home or parents. But I knew that my family wasn't going to get better if nobody did anything about it.

Two days after I spoke to my teacher, my brothers, my sisters, and I were taken out of our home and separated—my older sister and my brothers to one home, my twin and I to another. When the social worker came, my brothers were crying, but I had no tears.

I didn't think I'd stay in foster care long. I thought the social worker would kick my dad out and help my mom. I thought my mom would get us out of foster care when everything at home was OK again. I also thought that I could see my parents and that they would be able to see that I cared that they get better. I hoped my mother would call me at my foster home and tell me that she was happy that I would try to get help for her and my dad. I wanted her to make me feel that none of this was my fault.

But when I called my mom, she told me that she hated me and that she wished I wasn't born. I felt that I could never love her again.

After that, I didn't speak to my parents for a long time. I didn't hear from them when I turned 15. They didn't make any attempt to get us out of the system. And when I heard that my mom was still using crack, I knew that she wasn't going to do anything. Much of me had believed that my parents would forgive me, but there was a little hole in my heart telling me that they never would.

At times I'd go to see my parents. But when I went to visit, my mom didn't say anything to me and my dad wanted to see me in private to abuse me. It was just the same as when I lived at home.

When I turned 16, I saw my mom for the last time. She brought cake and ice cream to my group home, but she made a face that told me she didn't want to be there. She looked angry. I didn't want to think about our past but she made me face reality.

"Tracey, can you come here?" she said. I didn't want to go in the other room, because I knew that she would tell me something to hurt my feelings.

"What's the matter?" was all that I could say.

"I'm still upset. You had a good family, and you went off and told those secrets. How could you?"

I didn't move. There was something inside that was trying to get out. When it finally did, I said, "Mom, I don't understand what the problem is. I'm glad that I told. It was better than watching you and dad get high all day, and letting dad just hurt me and you didn't do anything."

My mom looked at me. She didn't say a word. I was surprised. Then she turned away, gave me her back, and left.

When my mother left I knew I had lost something. I'd lost my family and I'd lost hope. Every part of me had wanted to believe that my parents would get the help they needed. But I could tell that my coming into care hadn't helped them at all.

Every part of me had wanted to believe that my parents would get the help they needed. But I could tell that my coming into care hadn't helped them at all.

To be betrayed by my mother felt like getting stabbed in the back. I'd always felt that my mom was my world. For so long I had wanted to move back home with her (if she had the guts to leave my dad). It made me so sad that I couldn't see her anymore, and I felt guilty—I still do—for telling on my parents.

I also felt angry that my mother didn't give a damn about anybody except her husband and her drugs. I can't forgive her, but I can understand why she did the drugs and tried to keep it a secret. It's hard to blame her because I know that life is hard and sometimes we do things to try to make it easier.

Giving up on my mom is hard, because it means giving up on my dream to go home and live my life the way I wanted it to be—happy and calm. I miss the way she used to dance with us. But if my mother couldn't see how she'd hurt my sister and me, then it would hurt me again to go home. If I lived with my mom I would have to fake it to the point that I would be back where I started, back to my silent ways.

It's also scary because now I have to be myself, not my mom's reject or my dad's slave, but myself. I don't know if I'm ready to do that. I usually feel most like myself when I can take care of something or somebody, like my sister. Then I feel like I'm still wanted. But I feel lost when my sister asks me a question about the things that happened to us. I can't talk to her about the past because I've pushed it away and it's too painful to bring back.

I always tried to hide my feelings in my head, but lately they are coming out with all of the rage and the hatred I couldn't express before. Sometimes out of nowhere it feels like the abuse is happening again. It's frightening. I feel like I've lost control of myself, because sometimes when my emotions come back I feel like I'm still in the past, not here, and I can't stop it.

Giving up on my mom is hard, because it means giving up on my dream to go home and live my life the way I wanted it to be—happy and calm.

It makes me feel weak that I can't seem to handle my own problems anymore. I want to stay under control and I don't want to get angry, because when I get angry I feel like I'm going to jump into hurting anybody that gets in my way. I fear that I might hurt somebody like my parents hurt me, and not realize it. Or I might hurt myself even if I know I don't want to.

One way I'm dealing with those feelings is therapy. At first I just thought the therapist was trying to get in my business. But when I started to go I found that I could talk about some of my problems, although I keep many secrets. What I do tell her feels good, like I'm getting my issues off my chest.

I've also started to take medication, although at first I was afraid I'd end up like my mom. Her medications made her look like she was always lost and didn't see the days end or begin. But I think the medication I'm taking is helping.

I've also tried to mourn the loss of my parents by writing poems and drawing. I can tell that I'm feeling less attached to my mom now. I don't worry about her as much as I did when I came into care, when I worried that she wouldn't be able to do the things that I did, like cooking, washing the dishes, and taking out the garbage.

Mostly I let go of my feelings by crying, although after I cry I feel like I don't know why I did that. My tears don't roll, they come down like the rain, and they don't stop. I fear that one day I'll cry and won't ever stop. To make myself feel better I go outside and I sit by the water.

One place I love to go is a small park along the river. I go there to let go of my feelings. I can cry down there without anybody trying to ask what's wrong. Sometimes I lie in the grass and forget where I am, even if there are people all around me. The water takes the sun and breaks it into little pieces that fly off in all directions. I look over at New Jersey and wonder if there's someone over there doing the same thing as me.

To the right I see the George Washington Bridge. I look at the cars and I wish that I were in one of those cars, riding away from my group home and away from my past. I see people around me looking at the sky and doing the same thing I'm doing: drifting. Then I get up. It's time to leave. So I walk away, and leave my feelings there.

The author was 17 when she wrote this story.
The following year she received a national journalism award
for one of her stories. She later attended college.

Jolie Prom

Parent to Your Parents?

By T. M.

Many kids like me feel like it's their responsibility to take care of their addicted parents, or wonder what they did wrong to make their parents hurt them. I talked about this with Toni Heinemann, a therapist in San Francisco who also runs the Children's Psychotherapy Project, which provides therapy to children in foster care. She tackled the questions I had that seemed impossible to answer.

Q: Why do kids sometimes feel they have to take care of their parents?

A: Little kids think the world revolves around them and that they're responsible for everything. Kids blame themselves. And they take care of parents because they wish for them to get better.

It's hard for all of us to say that there are limits to what we can do. We have a hard time saying, "There's nothing I can do about this problem."

Q: How does it affect kids to take the parents' role?

A: They have to grow up fast, and it makes kids angry. Because they're doing work they aren't supposed to be doing, and they figure out that they've been cheated. We all feel bad when we realize we've been cheated.

Q: When I was taken away from my parents, I felt useless, like I had no value. Why is that?

A: Sometimes when one person in a relationship has a problem (like abusing drugs, or being violent), the other person in the relationship can get so involved in trying to solve the person's problem that their life revolves around the other person. They can feel like they have no value if they're not helping the other person or easing their pain, even if they're getting hurt in the relationship. That's called a co-dependent relationship.

You could be the most perfect, wonderful kid in the whole world and that would not change your parents.

If you're feeling like, "I'm not living my life, I'm living this other person's life," a little bell should go off for you to say, "Uh-oh. This isn't good." A relationship should have room for both people and their interests.

Q: How can teens like me deal with feeling empty?

A: It's going to happen over time. Really, that has to do with being able to separate yourself from family. It's recognizing that your parents couldn't take care of you because of who they were, not because there was something wrong with you.

That's a common feeling—if I were good enough, worthy enough, my parents would have risen to the occasion. You could be the most perfect, wonderful kid in the whole world and that would not change your parents.

Q: How does it affect kids if their parents never get their lives together?

A: Well, it makes them mad, and scared that they'll follow the same path. It makes them really sad. It makes them feel sorry for their parent. Or they feel like the world is against them.

It's important to keep in mind the whole picture. Lots of times, when parents aren't able to get their lives together, there's lots of contributors: poverty, racism, poor education, or their own childhood abuse. It's not only that their parents don't have the will to do it, it's also a societal problem.

Q: How can teens move on?

A: Painfully, but probably by finding people who do have their lives together—a mentor, a teacher. And keep an opening in your heart so that you that you can move on, but if a parent does get better, there's space for that relationship again.

Q: Why do some kids end up turning to drugs?

A: Sometimes people feel overwhelmed and they don't know what to do to feel better and they see this is something that people do to feel better. Or they think, "I can be different, I can use a little bit, I'm not going to be hooked."

They want immediate relief. It's hard to get yourself out of bed every morning and get to school in order to have a better life. If you haven't developed the skills to manage your emotions, you take the easy way out.

Q: Do all kids end up like their parents?

A: No. They don't. They find other people who can show them other ways of managing problems—you can write about it, talk to friends, go for a walk, reach out for help, and take help that's offered. Sometimes it's right there to be taken.

The author was 17 when she conducted this interview.

Terrance Taylor

Making It on My Own

By D.B.

My mom is a drug addict. Growing up in Watts my life was hell, because while she did drugs I had to help her get through her days.

Starting when I was 8, I got my mom food, laid her clothes out on the bed, helped her brush her teeth, and ran her bath water. I also did all the duties that a mother is supposed to do, like feeding my little sister and two brothers, making them take a bath, and getting them to school. It's been hard not having a mother who takes care of me and is there for me, but I learned to make it on my own.

Growing up, I went to elementary school only about once every three weeks because I had to take care of my siblings. My friends would ask me, "Why don't you go to school?" and I'd say, "I don't have time." I would walk away before they could ask why. Later I would talk to my friends through a window at home and they would tell me what went on in school.

The little girl inside me had it hard. I didn't go outside to ride my bike, skate, or talk to my friends. I knew that if I went outside at 5 p.m., I would have to come back inside at 6 to cook dinner. I wished I could play with the other kids on my block. They looked like they were having fun.

The hardest part was when my mom asked me to go next door to buy her drugs, like weed, methamphetamine, and cocaine. She was often too tired to do it herself. I wanted to die because I felt like it would be my fault if she overdosed. But I did it so she wouldn't yell at me.

When I was around 9 I decided I could not be my mom's drug supplier anymore. Sometimes when I refused to get her drugs she screamed at me and called me a "worthless piece of s—t." I'd fake laugh and say, "Ha-ha. You're funny." I thought that drugs made her do things she didn't really mean to, so back then it didn't even make me angry.

Everything changed when I was 11. A lady from the Department of Children and Family Services came to my school and took away my little sister and me. She told me, "The school called us and said that you and your sister have not been in school and that your mom has a major drug problem." I began to cry.

Little did I know I would never move back home. I went through two different foster homes before, at age 13, I moved with my sister to a group home in Hollywood called Aviva.

Living in a group home was tough because I had to live with 50 other girls. The staff told us what time to wake up, go to school, eat, and go to sleep. I was used to doing whatever I wanted. I was mad at everything: my mom, the system. I took my anger out on anybody.

One day I got in an argument with a supervisor and I socked her. That night, I got in another fight because a girl didn't clean up her mess when I asked. The staff sent me to my room.

In my room, I met a new girl named Lapondra. Lapondra told me about how she had to do everything for herself because her mom used drugs. But she didn't let her past get to her. She had struggled but she kept her head up. She told me, "Whatever doesn't kill you makes you stronger." Lapondra inspired me to be more positive and love myself for who I am.

The staff at Aviva kept bugging me to call my mom. They told me, "She's probably worried about you." Most of the girls saw their families on the weekends, but not me. I wondered if my mom had stopped doing drugs and if she wanted to see me or hug me.

But I hadn't called her since I went into the system. I was afraid she would hate me for not being there to clean up the house. I started thinking that maybe I should call her. Maybe she really was thinking about me.

The hardest part was when my mom asked me to go next door to buy her drugs. I felt like it would be my fault if she overdosed.

Finally, I picked up the phone and called my mom. I couldn't even talk because I was crying. My mom asked why I had to be so far away. That felt weird because she had never asked me questions like that. When I was at home she'd never asked me simple stuff to show she cared, like, "Where are you going?" or, "Where have you been?" It made me feel good.

But then she asked me, "When are you going to buy me a Scooby Doo sweater?" I couldn't believe it. She said, "You get a check every month."

I said, "Never!" and hung up the phone. I went to my room and cried. My mom had been talking slowly and I figured she was still doing drugs. I didn't even know if she was caring for my younger brother.

I still had a lot of anger inside. I got into another fight and eventually had to leave Aviva. I went to another group home called Penny Lane. I still had an "I don't care" attitude, and I got into a big fight right away.

I got scared that I would be sent to jail if I got in a fight again, so I talked to one of the staff, Damon. He gave me lectures about my behavior and how I could better myself. He told me I didn't have to whine like the other kids when I didn't get my way. It reminded me of what Lapondra told me about holding your head up and being positive.

I wanted a normal relationship, with a mom who tells you to go to school and gives you attention.

After that, my behavior started to improve. What also helped was going to an anger management group. It was difficult at first because I didn't want to remove the anger I had inside. I felt that if I changed, people would look at me differently. But a little part of me thought it might help. I was tired of losing my voice screaming at everybody. I learned that when I get mad, I don't have to go off. I can go to my room, turn on my music, and write in my journal. That worked. Gradually, I stopped getting into fights.

The day after my 15th birthday, on the spur of the moment, I called my mom. I wanted a normal relationship, with a mom who tells you to go to school and do your homework and gives you attention. A mom who would tell me, "You'll come home some day."

Even though my mom said some nice things, it didn't go well. I told her I hated her because I blamed her for my being in the system. She told me I had to get away from her to have a better life and that I was still her angel. She told me, "Don't worry, you'll be home soon."

But somehow, that wasn't enough. I thought it was a lie and that she never cared about me. If I tried to tell her about my problems, she said, "Oh girl, don't worry about that." I felt that she didn't take my life seriously.

After that I decided not to talk to my mom anymore. I was trying to better myself, but I realized that whenever I talked to my mom, she brought me down and made me feel like crap. We barely knew each other and we didn't understand each other. And I'm still angry at her for using drugs.

These days I try not to think about my mom that much, and I won't contact her. For now, it's easier that way. It hurts that I don't have a real mother-daughter relationship. But if it's not possible to have a normal relationship, then I have to focus on making things better for myself.

When I was younger, I thought I would end up addicted to drugs like my mom. But I'm doing better than I expected because of the foster care system. Being in the system hasn't always been a good thing, but it kept me in school. I'm going to graduate from high school and I plan on going to college. I'm proud of that. Even though life has been hard, I feel like I'm going to make it.

The author wrote this story for LA Youth, a newspaper by and for teens in Los Angeles. Copyright © LA Youth. Reprinted with permission.

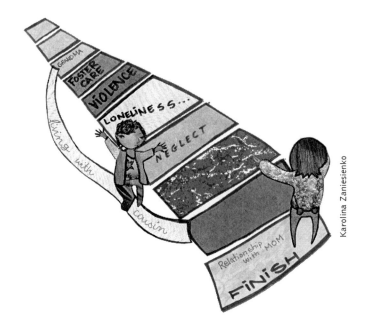

Karolina Zaniesienko

A Second Chance

By Karen Haynesworth

When I was little I would sit in my room and wonder why my life was not like other children's. I would see kids with their parents, doing things that my mother would not do with me, like going to the park and shopping, and I would feel sad.

I used to see my mother more often, and we would do those things together. Our relationship was good. But after I got a little older she would just come and go.

My grandmother, my mother, and I all lived together, so my grandmother usually looked after me when my mother wasn't there. My grandmother would try to take her place by taking me shopping, to the movies, and to the park. That was OK but I also wanted my mother to take me places. I wanted to bond with the person I came from. I often asked my grandma, "Where is Mom?" She would not answer me. It would be the same thing day after day.

Then one day my grandmother answered. I saw my mother and I asked her to stay with me. My mother said, "I have to handle some business."

I asked, "Handle what?" She ignored me and left.

I turned to Grandma. "Grandma, what business does Mom have to handle?"

She said, "Your mother takes drugs."

I didn't know what to say.

She continued, "I'm tired of not saying nothing. You were going to find out someday."

I always wondered why my mother was not taking care of her responsibility to raise me. Now I knew. But I didn't like the information. I began to get upset. I wished my grandmother had told me the truth sooner. I also felt that my mother didn't want me as much as she wanted her drugs. If she did, she would not be spending more time with them than me.

Soon my mother's addiction got worse. Every night she came home high or drunk and I could tell. She would slur her words and be hard to understand. Then, when I was 9, my grandmother was no longer able to take care of me, so the city decided to put me in a foster home. I knew my life was going to change completely.

I was sad that I had to leave my grandmother, my mother, and my siblings, who stayed with my grandmother because they had special needs that couldn't get met in a regular foster home. I still wanted to be with them. They were my family, but I had to go.

But I was also hopeful. I felt Children's Services might be getting me out of a bad situation, since my mother did drugs. So I went in the foster home thinking that I would be safe and the foster parents would give me the support and stability I did not always get at home. I was wrong.

The foster parents treated me even worse. My mother never abused me, but the foster parents hit me and their children bit and kicked me. They also said that I was going to be nothing, just like my mother, and that that's why I was in every other home but hers. That made me angry to hear. I still loved my mother, even if I didn't live with her.

Eventually I was moved, but most of the places I was moved to weren't a whole lot better. For many years I suffered physical and mental abuse from foster parents, and for many years I missed my family. All of this affected me badly. I did not want to talk to anyone. I spent most of the time alone in my room.

I went into care thinking that I'd be safe and get the support and stability I did not always get at home. I was wrong.

During visits with my family, I wouldn't tell them what was happening in the foster homes. I thought I'd get in trouble with the foster parents if I did.

I saw my mother every two weeks. I was always excited to see her at our visits. She'd get to the agency first to surprise me. She would bring me lots of toys and gifts. When it was my birthday, she had a birthday party for me at the agency. She decorated the room with balloons and I had a big cake.

It felt so good to see her. Whenever my mother was around, something in my heart felt complete. Just her being around made me happy. My mother never missed a visit and she always said she loved me no matter what.

But when I was 11, she stopped coming. Later I found out that she hadn't been attending her court dates, and she lost her rights to see me. But at the time I did not understand what was wrong. All I knew was that my mother stopped showing up. My grandmother would bring my brother and sisters and sometimes my cousin Michelle instead. I felt happy to see them, but sad and upset that my mother was not there too.

My grandmother was a mother figure to me and I loved her

dearly, but when the visits were over my mind would go right back to thinking about not seeing my mother, how much I missed her, and when I might see her again. I wanted her to be there for me. This was the hardest time for me. But even through this, I never felt my mother did not love me. Every time I saw her, she had said she did.

Though I never talked about my troubles, during agency visits my cousin Michelle saw that I was suffering, maybe because I never really talked. As I got older, like 13, I began to get closer to her. Michelle was 25 and had two children of her own. She began to talk with me about moving in her home.

Michelle was still in college, working on her teaching degree, when she decided her mind was set to help me. So after school she attended training classes at the agency to become my foster parent. I felt happy about that, because no one else in my family was willing to go through all of the agency's training.

When she got certified, I moved into Michelle's home. I was going to be with my family and it wouldn't be at the agency. That felt so good.

My cousin made me feel like I was at home by letting me know I was safe. At first, I would do strange things like put my arm around my plate so no one would take my food from me. I would also stay long periods of time in my room by myself. Even though I was happy to be home, part of me was still missing my mother, so I would sit alone and think mainly about her.

My cousin helped me overcome these problems. She would move my hand from around my plate, saying, "I am not going to take your food away from you, you can eat as much as you want here." She would take me with her to the store and spend time with me so I wouldn't feel alone.

I gradually became more open and more able to trust people. Michelle showed me that caring for someone does not come from abuse. When I did something wrong she would not hit me, she would put me on punishment or she would talk to me. She did not choose her children over me. We were all treated equally.

My cousin became my role model. She showed me the right path and helped change my life. She taught me that I have to work for what I want if I want the best in life. She also taught me how to put my education first, because without an education, I won't get far.

But maybe most important, even though the agency did not allow me visits with my mother, Michelle allowed me to have a relationship with her. She thought it was important for my mother to get to know me and for me to know her.

The first time my mother came to my cousin's apartment I felt so happy. I gave her the biggest hug and kiss. It was like a part of my heart was still cut, but when I saw her it healed. I even forgot I had not seen her for so long. She looked like the same person I had stopped seeing at the agency—her appearance never changed to me. That's how much I loved and missed her.

I know I am not going to live with my mother again, but I am happy to have a relationship with her.

As I got older and as we spent more time together, I started to tell my mother about the problems I had faced in the foster homes. I wanted her to know what I had been through. She got upset anytime I told her they mistreated me. She said, "I am sorry you had to go through this. You don't have to worry anymore because Michelle will take good care of you."

As we began to bond more we talked about the problems she had to deal with. I learned that what started her on drugs was that some of my brothers died in a fire before I was born. She couldn't take the pain and turned to drugs.

When we talked about these things, my mother admitted that she had a problem with drugs and that she struggled to get clean. I respected her for saying that and it meant a lot to me to hear. Some people who are addicted to drugs won't admit it's a problem. Some won't own up to how their problem has hurt their children. My mother did both, and it was good for me to know who she really is, and to understand why she had such a hard time taking care of me.

I know I am not going to live with my mother again, but I am happy to have a relationship with her. It's important to me, not just to know where I came from, but to also bond with a person I have so much in common with. I only have one mother, even if someone else raises me.

I don't live with my cousin anymore because she recently got married and I don't get along with her husband. But the five years we lived together put me on the right path—I graduated from high school and started college this fall, studying nursing. I still see my cousin and my mother even though I'm in a new foster home. (My new foster mother gives me the freedom to visit them.)

My mother has recovered from doing hard drugs. She went to a drug program every week to quit. I know it was hard for her because getting away from drugs is not easy for anybody, but she was willing to fight.

Somehow I have managed to not hold a grudge against her for not being able to raise me, maybe because she seems truly apologetic that she couldn't do it for me, and because I understand a little bit about the pain she was going through with my brothers' deaths that made it hard for her to cope.

We have a good relationship and it's still growing. We see each other every weekend. I let her know I forgive her for what she did, but that does not mean I will ever forget what happened and what I've been through. I believe God has given our family a chance to start over.

Karen was 18 when she wrote this story.

Gabriel Appleton

I Bounced

By Anonymous

He opens the door, leaning on it for support. His voice is raspy and his bloodshot eyes speak of desperation. They're half-shut as he slurs the words, "Where ya been?" I feel sorry for him.

As I take a deep breath, I'm surprised that my brother doesn't smell like a brewery today. He doesn't smell like anything. He asks why I moved out a few days before. "I've been staying with a friend because I don't appreciate people yelling at me, and I don't like yelling at other people," I reply in the politest voice I can think of. And in the most sober voice he can find, he says, "Nobody was yelling at ya, you were yelling at yourself."

My brother knows why I left, but he won't admit that it was partly his fault. He dropped out of high school two months before his graduation, but that wasn't his fault either; the principal didn't like him. He has two sons that aren't his fault; that's why he doesn't pay child support.

I'm not sure how any of these "explanations" for what's wrong in his life make any sense. But that's the way it is with alcoholics and drug addicts.

All my life I've struggled to separate myself from the substance abusers in my family. Just about everyone in my family has had a problem with drinking or drugs. My brother's an alcoholic. My sister smokes crack. My mother doesn't care how much she drinks. Even my father has had drug problems in the past, but at least he's always been there for me. Unknowingly, my family backed me up against a wall and made me climb over it to escape.

While I was growing up, my parents fought constantly—once to the point that my father moved to the trashy first floor of the house. I would give him my dinner because he wasn't eating. Then he disappeared. He headed to his parents' house when things got too rough. Unfortunately, he also headed to crack.

At 11 years old, I didn't want to believe Mommy when she said that Daddy smoked crack. I refused to accept that another person in my family was falling apart. Especially not Daddy. Not the Daddy who sang "Amazing Grace" with me on our road trips to Maine and told me I was good company because I kept him awake.

He's the one who showed me that I deserve more than my family offers, even though he was working 10 hours a day, six days a week. When he disappeared for weeks at a time because of drugs, I let him come back and become Daddy all over again. If I didn't forgive him, I had no one. And neither did he, because I was his only "cub"—my other four siblings have a different father.

Out of my siblings, my sister was my favorite because she took me to the mall and bought me anything I wanted. My sister was best at breaking away and getting attention, so I took lessons from her. She needs to feel loved, and loves to feel needed.

But as a young child I never understood why she'd always take me to the "bad part" of Connecticut to get her "candy." And why did I have to hide under the dashboard? When she went to jail, it tore me apart inside. I felt like a piece of me was being locked away where I wouldn't be able to find it for a very long time.

Then, last July, she said she needed to get away from her boyfriend, so she came to stay with me and my family. She brought with her a bottle of whiskey and a few bags of clothes. One night, she walked into my room, drinking from her precious bottle. Calmly, I said, "Laura, you can do whatever you want to do, just don't do it around me." She apologized and left.

I didn't think it was fair that she drank and used drugs, and was always forgiven. She dropped out of school and ran away when she was 12, but could always come and become the life of the party again. I resented her for it and loved her for it at the same time. She is adventurous, but stupid. Smart, but terribly ignorant. Her life's mistakes have become my life's lessons.

Two weeks later she said she missed her boyfriend and left. As I was cleaning around the bed she slept in, I found a strange object. It looked like a small pipe, with burnt aluminum foil held onto the base by a rubber band. There was a hole leading to the body of a Paper-Mate pen, all brown on the inside.

I finally realized that it was a homemade crack pipe. The flakes of burnt powder on the foil described my sister's escape. I knew it. I had always known she was using drugs, I just prayed that it wasn't true. But there was no way to deny it now—my sister was addicted to crack.

I brought the pipe to my mother, who sat at her new piano, her pride and joy, playing Chopin. She just finished another glass of wine, and was nonchalant when she informed me that she and my brother had found the pipe a week ago. The shock took a second to wear off. When it did, I was disgusted by how normal this all seemed to her. She made it seem like it was all OK; but it wasn't.

I knew what I had to do. I took the pipe and the whiskey bottle my sister left behind and went outside. In my pajamas I walked down to the pier at the end of the street. The wind made my wet hair feel cold as it slapped my face.

With all my anger I threw the bottle on the rocks and it smashed into hundreds of pieces. The smell of whiskey filled the air while the wind escorted me to the end of the dock, where I took apart the pipe and heaved it into the Eerie Basin. That was my final stand.

I felt completely broken. I thought, "What do I do now? I've just rebelled against the only people I have to depend on." I wanted support but I had nowhere to look for it, except the place that I despised so dearly: home. I gave up and returned to find my mother and brother sharing a six-pack of Budweiser. I was clinging to the hands that beat me.

I was desperate to separate myself from my family.

I told my brother what happened and he said, "Yeah, well, we all know Laura smokes crack, it's not a new thing. I drink, Laura does drugs, Peter smokes weed. I'm sorry if we all can't be perfect like you." This comment hurt me more than it should have. I felt like I cut off all emotion toward them. He was explaining that he and my mother were the norm, while I was the freak. So I took my freak self upstairs to be alone.

The blankets I had thrown on the floor called to me. They offered protection and support. Comfort without fear. More than I ever got from my family. They engulfed me, tempted me to give up.

I wanted to drink and smoke, lie, cheat, and steal. But would that make me feel better? Would I be happier if I was weak? No. I needed to be strong.

"I have the better father, therefore, I've had the better upbringing," I thought to myself. My father had cleaned up his life and showed me I can escape from the negativity of my family.

"I know what I want to do when I get older, therefore, I have a goal. I need to reach my goals," I thought. I've had to help myself most of my life. I've become strong because of it. My life has been a struggle to prove that it is possible to break the cycle.

Luckily, soon after that day I went to Maine for a couple weeks of vacation. At first, I felt so angry I thought, "I just don't care about them anymore. I'm showing the same amount of affection and kindness they always showed me. Absolutely none."

Then I realized that I could continue to resent my family, and rebel against them, but my anger would only tear me up inside while they lived on in their ignorant worlds of denial. In the end, I decided to forgive them, and came back feeling peaceful and mature.

My mother and I didn't argue for six weeks, until I told her I had decided to join the army. I was desperate to separate myself from my family, and the army offered me that escape.

I refused to accept that another person in my family was falling apart.

However, my mother didn't react well to my good news. She didn't understand why I wanted to do the one thing that could save me from Red Hook, Brooklyn. She is always so good at ignoring what I do to make myself better than those around me, and I felt tired of it.

We got in a fight, but instead of confronting her directly, I threw a trophy at her piano, leaving two dents in the side, like a vampire bite. Later, I apologized to my mother for the damage, but that wasn't enough.

The next day my brother woke me up at 9 a.m. so he could punish me for defacing my mother's property. I was getting out of control, he said, and needed to be "straightened out."

All my life I was "straightened out" in a very painful way. I've called the police on my brother before, after his misguided attempts to discipline me. He never understood that getting beaten won't make me behave "better." And I will not be "straightened out" anymore.

My mother finally convinced my brother to leave me alone. But I was so mad, I needed to take my anger out on someone. I opened healing wounds by telling her that I'm her only hope of having some sort of successful child. I was in a rage, and the last thing I said to my mother was, "You're lucky I don't beat you like your son did me, and you're lucky I don't burn your damn piano!"

I ran to my friend's house two blocks away and rang her bell at 9:30 a.m. I explained the morning's events, and she said, "Forget your mother, what did she ever do for you?" She knew that I needed to stay somewhere away from my family for the next two months until I left for basic training, so she offered to let me stay at her house (in return for leaving my computer with her). I finally had a solid opportunity to make the physical break from my family that I had already made emotionally. I was finally leaving home for good.

It's easier to cope with my family now that I have the choice whether or not I want to. I still see my mother about once a week. I feel like I don't need my family, but I feel obligated to stay connected to them. They've taught me so much by pushing me away. I've learned the importance of being on my own.

So I'm sitting here on my temporary bed, in my temporary room, typing this story on my temporary computer, waiting until I can finally escape.

The author was in high school when she wrote this story.

© Make a Better Place

Doing Time in the Hood

By Lakia Holmes

When I was 12, I was placed in a foster home because my mother was a drug addict. She had been one since her late teens. She would binge on crack for hours, sometimes days on end, then sleep for a day or two.

Because of this, I never really had a childhood. Just about everything I learned I taught myself. While my friends were worrying about what game to play during lunchtime, I worried about whether or not I was going to eat that day.

Social workers from children's services took me out of school and placed me in a foster home in Brooklyn, New York, far away from my mom's home in Harlem, in Manhattan. I was all alone— no friends, no family, no nothing.

Normally I'm a person who doesn't mind being alone, but being alone in a new neighborhood was scary. I mean, before then I had never even been in Brooklyn. Imagine that you're from Los Angeles, and someone just picks you up and drops you in, say, Boise, Idaho, then says, "This is your new home." How would you feel? Probably just as scared as I was.

But about three weeks later, I got the news that I thought would make a difference. After school, I heard my foster mother talking on the phone to my social worker. It sounded as if they were making plans. Then I heard something about 152nd Street and St. Nicholas Place. Streets of my old neighborhood!

After my foster mother hung up the phone, she told me what I felt like I'd been waiting for my whole life. (Really I'd just been waiting a few weeks.) I was going back to Manhattan! One of my mother's best friends was a foster parent, and she lived on the exact same block I used to live on. I would be moving in with her. I would still get to see my friends and still go to my old school. A happiness came over me like never before.

A couple of weeks later I moved into my new home. Everything was going well. My foster parents were great to me. They let me hang out with my friends, they bought me things, they just treated me better than my mother did.

But there were still the same old problems in my neighborhood. My neighborhood is probably like many others throughout the country. On the outside, it looks like your typical block, nice houses, friendly people, most of whom are very hard-working middle-class folk who look like they have not a care in the world.

But on the inside, some of those nice houses and friendly people hold dark secrets, like my mom's home did. Drugs and alcohol were a big part of those secrets.

Still, this neighborhood was my home. I wanted to believe that the problems that I faced when I was living with my mother wouldn't affect me in my new foster mother's home. When I was little and visited my foster mother's house with my mother, I would feel a strange sense of security there, maybe because they paid attention to me and acted as if they cared about me. I felt safe, something I always wanted when I was living with my mother.

But as time went by, problems started to arise in my new home, too. My foster parents drank and took drugs like my mom. Now this was no surprise to me. I mean, I had known them since I was a baby. When I would go there to visit, I would see them have a drink or two, and then they would smoke a joint or two. OK, maybe more than two, but I was young. I didn't know that drugs and alcohol were bad. In fact, I thought that smoking crack or weed was as common as brushing your teeth in the morning.

But living with them I began to realize how big their problem was. They would drink huge bottles of liquor as if they were water. Instead of bacon and eggs for breakfast, they'd drink vodka. I found it surprising that my social worker never smelled alcohol on my foster mother's breath, and didn't notice when she was drunk. I guess my foster mother was good at hiding it.

I thought that smoking crack or weed was as common as brushing your teeth in the morning.

But as my awareness of the drinking rose, that strange sense of security became stranger and then it began to drift away. When both my foster parents were drunk, they'd start to argue, mostly about how my foster mother wasn't "satisfying" my foster father. My foster mother would tell him to go find someone else to do it, and he did. He chose me.

I was about 14 when it started. He would blow kisses at me, lick his lips and stroke his crotch. He began to make my already complicated life even more complicated. He made serious advances toward me on several occasions. After each time, I blamed it on the alcohol. I figured that after he realized I was rejecting his advances he would stop. Then he told me that he could not wait until I was old enough so he could have sex with me and get away with it. That's when I knew it was not going to stop.

And it didn't, but it did seem to slow down after a few

months. I started thinking, "Well, maybe he sees that I'm not giving in to him." But come to find out, he had found another victim in the unlikeliest of places: my mother.

My mother had gotten evicted from her apartment. My foster mother didn't want to see her out on the street, so she decided to let my mother stay with us for a while. This was very illegal. The only time I was supposed to see my mother was at the agency for supervised visits.

But now both my mother and I were living in my foster home. And now my mother and my foster mother were doing drugs in my supposedly safe foster home. Every time my social worker came for home visits, my mother would either hide in the back of the house, where the social worker would never go, or she would leave before my social worker came.

So now I'm thinking, "They took me from one drug-infested home, put me in another drug-infested home, and the person who made my first drug-infested home infested is living in my new drug-infested home making it even more infested." There's only so much infestation a person can take.

Anyway, one night my mother was sleeping in my room and I woke up to a commotion. My mother and foster father were yelling at each other. My foster father was now trying to force himself on my mother. "Stop!" she yelled. "Stop!"

"Come on, you know you want it as much as I do," he said.

I don't know how far my foster father got with my mother, and although I had a lot of animosity toward my mother, it hurt me to hear what was going on. You're probably saying, "Well, why didn't you tell your social worker?" I wanted to, but I didn't want to go through the trouble of being placed in a new home far away. I felt that I couldn't handle the emotional stress of leaving my neighborhood. Trying to meet new people and having to adjust to a new parent's rules and attitude was a little more than I thought I could take.

My little brother, who was living with me, was another reason why I didn't want to leave. He had become attached to our home and to our foster parents, plus he got to see our biological mother all the time. I thought that if he lost all that he could've lost his mind, because he was only 3.

But if moving would've been hard, living there wasn't easy either. For some reason, I started to believe that everything going on was my fault. If I stayed, my foster father would keep sexually harassing me and my mother, and it would be my fault for not doing anything about it. If I told, then my family would say that it was my fault for being placed somewhere else.

And what if I did tell my social worker and she didn't believe me? That would mean that I'd have to face a whole new set of problems.

I stayed there for about two more years, and during that time my whole world changed. My grades dropped so much that if there was a grade below F, I probably would have gotten it. I started cutting class, shoplifting, and doing other things that I normally wouldn't do. I started thinking about committing suicide, and then I started to try it.

My grades dropped so much that if there was a grade below F, I probably would have gotten it.

I also began doing things that I knew would bother my family, just for the pleasure of seeing them mad. When I was mad they didn't ask me what was wrong or even say, "You'll be all right," so I figured that I'd make them suffer by causing trouble.

One day I went to the local drug store and stole a little tube of lip gloss—or I should say I tried to steal a little tube of lip gloss. As I walked through the door, two undercover cops stopped me. If it wasn't for my age, they probably would have arrested me, and that's when I knew something had to change. I figured that if I stayed in that home I would wind up hurting myself, someone else, or wind up in jail, whichever came first.

I finally decided that I needed to go to another home. To make that happen, I told my grandmother about the sexual abuse. She gave me the reassurance I needed and said that she would call the agency. A few weeks went by. I was waiting for the agency to call saying that they had found my brother and me a new place to stay. After another couple of weeks, I realized something had gone wrong.

Turns out, my grandmother had decided not to tell the agency because she didn't want my brother and me to move far away. Thank God for people who have their priorities in order!

Later on I found out that my grandmother also didn't believe me about the sexual abuse. Now, it's true that lying had practically become a second language to me, but why would I lie about being molested? I mean, going around and telling people that I was almost raped for the hell of it is not my idea of being funny!

Luckily, not too long after this I found out that someone told the agency about my foster mother's drug and alcohol abuse, and they decided that her home was unfit to be a foster home. I was sent to a home in Far Rockaway, Queens. I found that pretty ironic. I didn't want to be placed far away and they sent me to a place called Far Rockaway.

The neighborhood is a lot quieter, a lot safer, than my old one. At first it was weird to be there. I thought that I wouldn't like it, but now I wish that I'd spent my entire life here. I'm still with my brother, and my foster mother and her boyfriend treat us as if we're their own children. Now I don't worry about whether someone is going to come in my room in the middle of the night and harm me. I don't have to worry about staying in a drug-infested home, watching weed smoke fill up my house.

Going through the whole process of changing schools and meeting new people was hard but worth it. My grades are back up and I will be graduating on time. I do sometimes miss my friends and classmates and some of my relatives. Still, I've gained something worthwhile: peace of mind, which I've wanted for a long time.

After I moved to Far Rockaway, the agency felt I should go to therapy. I told my therapist about my past and she then told my new foster mother. My foster mother called my mother and grandmother and confronted them. (I was secretly listening on the other end.) My grandmother acted as if she knew nothing about what went on at my old house, even though I had told her. She called me crazy and said that I needed help. I felt that was the worst thing she had ever said about me. I mean, how dare she say that? She didn't know what I was going through, the pain and anguish I suffered. And to think that I put myself through all this because I wanted to be with her and I thought she wanted to be with me.

My grandmother would kill me if she ever heard me say this, but I'm going to say it anyway: I would be really angry if I had to leave my current foster home, especially if it was to go back to my grandmother or mother. In fact, if I wasn't so old, I'd ask my foster mother to adopt me. Unfortunately, I will be leaving my home soon, because in the fall I will be attending college upstate.

My grandmother acted as if she knew nothing about what went on at my old house, even though I had told her.

It's possible that if the system didn't put me back in my old neighborhood, I might have wound up in just as bad a foster home someplace else. But it's also possible that I would not have gone through the things I did. Maybe I would've had a more normal childhood. Maybe I wouldn't worry so much. I can't even imagine how many maybes or what ifs there are. I guess I'm just glad that eventually I did end up here, in Far Rockaway.

Lakia was 17 when she wrote this story. She later got her GED and attended college at Brigham Young University.

Stephanie "Meadow" Kunar

Starting Over Without Them

By Hattie Rice

When I was 13, I stopped going to school. The kids called me retarded and I had no friends. All I thought about was going home to play cards and watch TV with my mom. Being at home comforting my mom was a way to get away from the torment of school and to play my role in the family—daughter and psychiatrist to my mom.

I was afraid of leaving my mother alone. I worried that one day my problems (not liking people and stress, which were the problems she was aware of) and her problems (using drugs and hearing voices) would fall down on her and she'd die of stress.

I was 9 when my dad told me that he and my mom were schizophrenic. He was scared of people but could function. He was able to work. He said my mother had it worse. She heard voices and thought people were trying to drive her crazy and to kill her. To cope with the pain, she started smoking crack.

Soon her addiction started to show. She would steal money from the family. Sometimes we'd have no food in the house and would have to go to churches or beg at the welfare office. It made me feel embarrassed. I'd think, "This is not the way a kid should live, begging for food." I felt like she didn't care about me, because if she did, why would she spend our food money on crack?

Most of the time she was high and fidgety. When I touched her, she'd jump. Other times my mother would cry because of the voices and my dad would argue with her over her drug habit.

"You going to smoke up all the money," Dad would say.

"Please, just one more smoke," Mom would say.

My brother and I used to think, "Dad, why are you letting her do this to us?"

It's become obvious to me that my mom needs more help than a child can give.

When I stopped going to school, a typical day with my mom started with her using half of the food money on crack and then coming home and smoking it. I'd usually check on her (because I could hear her talking to the voices) and she'd tell me to tell the voices to stop hurting her. I'd say a prayer for her and we'd play her favorite card game or watch television while I held her.

Then I'd give her my usual lecture, telling her the voices are in her head and that other people aren't doing it to her. I'd make clear that I didn't want to hurt her. I'd tell her she has a mental illness. My mom would hold me and cry when I comforted her.

It was hard feeling responsible for her, and sometimes it was overwhelming because I had my own problems. I also felt it wasn't a child's place to take care of her mother.

It was especially confusing to know that my mom was not in control of the way she acted. When she took our money to buy crack, I knew it was because she felt she needed it to cope with her problems, or when I tried to touch her or get close and she'd fidget, it was because of her addiction.

I'd tell myself not to be upset, because she wasn't trying to hurt me. But as much as I tried to understand, I also felt angry and abandoned. Even now I don't think I can ever forgive my mom for spending the food money. I think to myself, "If you really loved me, why would you do that to me? You saw how I was suffering."

Over time I got depressed. When I woke in the morning, I didn't want to leave the house because I felt like the world had nothing to offer me. At home I would cry. My frustration made me start eating a lot. I used to weigh more than 185 pounds.

My mother doing drugs had me feeling like life wasn't worth living. Eventually I figured I should just stay at home and avoid the world.

When I stopped going to school, I didn't think anybody would realize I was gone, but the attendance office called ACS, the child welfare agency in New York City. ACS sent a social worker to inspect our house, which was not in good shape. Every time the social worker came I stayed in my room. I think he recommended counseling for me because I would never talk to him.

The psychiatrist diagnosed me as having social phobia and I ended up being taken away from my family because they failed to make me go to school and didn't get my psychiatric prescription filled.

When I entered foster care, I was terrified. The first week, I stayed in my room and cried day and night. It was strange not to wake up and watch TV or play video games, and to have nobody to say "I love you" to. I just wanted to go back home.

Being in care felt scary because I knew my mom had nobody to console her. My parents came to visit every weekend. I felt better then because we'd go out for a walk and my mom would cry on my shoulder just like the old days.

But I soon began to feel relieved that the weight of my family's problems had been lifted off my shoulders. I realized that caring for my mom was hurting my life. I think my mom is able to get along without me. Unfortunately, that's because she smokes crack to forget about life. I feel upset about that, but it's become obvious to me that she needs more help than a child can give.

As I got settled into my placement, I realized I wasn't getting all of the attention I needed at home and it felt good to focus on myself. There was not a lot of stress in the group home and if I needed someone to talk to there was always staff on duty. I felt good knowing I had staff that led me in the right way and girls that helped lift my spirits. That's when I started to think that foster care is where I need to be.

In the group home, I can focus on my education and try to deal with my fear of people before it gets worse. I've started interacting with the girls well (and that's never been one of my specialties) and opening up about the anger I felt toward my mom by telling a new friend what I'd been going through at home.

During the first year of living without my parents, my depression lifted tremendously. As I talked more about my feelings and let them out, I didn't wake up crying like I did at home and I lost the weight I gained.

I started to realize that the world has many wonderful things to offer me, because I started to go outside, hang out with my friends and have fun. I was even able to go back to school and keep up an 85 average.

I realized that my depression was caused by stress at home and my failure to be able to communicate with people at school and make friends. Now I know that the only worries I need to have are about me, myself and I. It feels great to feel stronger and in control.

On my home visits, I saw that home was not where I needed to be because I saw my family still arguing over why there's no food money. Then they'd ask me for money. I'd say, "I live in foster care and work a summer job. I ain't got no money."

I felt glad that I could go see them, but I also appreciated having the option to leave when things got too intense. I wanted to be close to my mom, to let her know I care for her and that she's not alone in this world, but I also felt like I needed to stay detached so her problems won't affect me the way they used to. Now when her problems become unbearable, it's back to my home away from home.

Not being surrounded by them has also me realize how mad I feel. I've always tried to cover up my feelings when I'm with my mom, because I figured that she has enough stress without knowing that she hurts me. But lately my feelings have been hurt so bad I can't cover them up, like when I think about how my mom and dad let us starve.

> *I felt glad that I could go see my parents, but I also appreciated having the option to leave when things got too intense.*

Then I blow up, screaming and yelling, "Shut the @#$% up and leave me the @#$% alone!" My mom will say, "MoMo (that's my nickname), what did I do to upset you? Why do you act like this? I love you." Instead of telling her what's wrong I'll hold her and say, "Sorry, I love you."

I only outburst once in a while but it makes me feel calm and refreshed to let my feelings out and to stand up to my mom and give her what she deserves. It's frightening, too, because sometimes I feel like I might never stop.

Since I came into foster care, I've realized how much it affects me to keep a lot of stuff held in me that I need to release. Sometimes I feel confused because I wonder, "Is it OK to feel sympathetic and angry at the same time? And if I always release the sympathetic side, where is all my anger going? And if I don't want to hurt my mother, when or how will I release my rage?"

Any blind man can see that my parents want me home, because they ask me, "When are you coming home?" and take me to my bedroom and ask me to spend a night. But whether they can actually care for me is the real question. (I think not, how about you?)

So after being in care for a year, I decided that going home would be a setback. The first person I told was my cousin. One day we were at my house and he asked me, "Do you want to come home?" Then he looked at me and added, "Who would want to come back here?" I said, "I sure as hell don't."

A few months ago, at a meeting with my parents, my social worker told my mom that I don't want to go home and my mom asked, "Is that true?" I said, "Yes." She asked, "Why, MoMo? We love you." Before she could start acting like a baby, my social worker cut her off. That day, my social worker also had my mom take a drug test. Of course she tested positive, so my social worker might try to convince her to get help.

I need to let her know I'm angry at her and that everything between us isn't peaches and cream.

When I left I felt good, because I felt like my mom needed to be rejected. I need to let her know I'm angry at her and that everything between us isn't peaches and cream. I feel like I'm being selfish, but I have to help myself.

I do have doubts about putting myself first, though. I wonder, "Who is my mom going to have?" And it's scary to focus on myself. Before, whenever I was confused or frustrated about my own problems, I could focus on my mom instead. Now I have nobody else's problems to get me away from my reality.

I don't think my parents really understand my decision to stay in foster care. And I think my mom is confused when I say that she's mistreated me, because she really can't seem to see what she did wrong.

For so long I never showed the way I feel about her, so I think my mom still does not understand that her drug habit affects me. Maybe the only way she'll understand is if I tell her straight up or call the police on her when she smokes or buys crack.

Right now, I think it's better for me to wonder what she knows than to know for sure, because I don't want to find out the answer. Maybe I'll have the courage to find out someday.

Hattie was 15 when she wrote this story.
She later graduated from high school and went to college.

Walter Moore

Man of the House

By Anonymous

We were in Guatemala, our usual vacation spot, in the summer of 2005. We had visited our relatives and seen many ancient ruins, beautiful lakes, and mountains. It was so much fun I asked my mom if we could stay longer.

"No, your father only has three weeks of vacation," she said.

"But we've still got two more weeks before school. Can we at least stay without him?" I begged. "Dad won't mind paying for our flights to be changed."

My mother laughed. "Go try and convince him," she said.

I easily persuaded my father to let my sister and me stay an extra two weeks with our family. Had I known this was going to be our last vacation, I would have asked to stay forever.

When I was younger I thought of my father as a very good person. He did everything he could to support my mom, my sister, and me. He helped all his friends and family when they asked him for it. He worked long hours as a limousine driver. I didn't see him much and we never really got a chance to talk because he was often asleep when I left for school and I was asleep when he came home from work. But I didn't mind because I knew he was working all those hours to provide for us.

My mother told me the reason he came home so late was because after work he would go out and drink. Then he would come home and not be able to sleep because he was throwing up. My mother hated to see him drink, but she told me she thought there were many reasons why he did it, like never getting over the death of his mother, and being treated unfairly as a child.

It didn't really bother me because I rarely saw him drink, and his alcohol use never seemed to disrupt his work or the family. At least not until the beginning of 2006, when I started to see changes in him.

My father began to drink more often and for the first time I began to witness it. I would come home from school to find him sitting on the couch watching TV, drinking a beer or already drunk. At first I thought he was just working an earlier shift, until it became a frequent habit. My father had always worked every day and only took his vacation in the summer, so why was he home more now?

I began to worry about money, as I was seeing less of it, but it wasn't something I spoke to him about. We hardly ever talked, and when we did, I felt he always tried to highlight the negative stuff I did and didn't acknowledge the good stuff. So I kept conversation to a minimum.

One day my parents had a huge fight. My mother said she was tired of putting up with him and she asked him to leave. So my father did just that. That night he told us he was going to live in his friend's basement and he would give us our money weekly. I felt relieved that I wouldn't have to come home and see him drunk anymore.

Later that night my mother told me the truth. My father was sick. He'd been diabetic since his youth, but because of his alcohol consumption he'd developed other illnesses associated with diabetes. His main problem was his sight. He was no longer able to see clearly from his right eye, even with his glasses, which is why he hadn't been working as much. My mom had kicked him out because he kept drinking and he wasn't contributing much toward the bills.

My father stayed away for about three months before my mother allowed him to come back. He could no longer work because with his bad eye he was now a threat on the road. My mom didn't have a job and we were just living off savings. It was only a couple of months before my parents had another huge argument and my father left once again.

Eventually, his problem spread to the other eye and he was forced to sell his car for money. He began losing weight, and every few weeks, when I dropped off mail for him, he looked worse. But he refused to move back in with us.

At first, I felt sorry for him. But then I found out that alcohol is a depressant and its users often turn to it because they want to get away from other problems. Even though I knew that alcoholism is a disease, I still felt the only one to blame was him. I was angry that he didn't seem to think of the trickling effect his alcoholism would have on his family.

Sometimes I wanted to express my feelings toward my father, but deep down I feared it would turn into violence, so I didn't. I thought to myself, "How could he just drink this whole time, knowing that it would be a time bomb that would eventually explode?"

What really got me mad was that nobody seemed to be doing anything about the situation. We had no money. Every day I would hear my mother talk about another bill that had come up. Meanwhile, my sister acted like nothing was wrong and seemed to be in denial about the fact that my father was no longer going to provide for us.

One day I started thinking about it and when my sister got home from school, she found me slamming doors. She came into the living room and asked me, "What's wrong?"

"Your father! Who does he think he is? Why would he do this to us?" I said.

"I don't know, but he still gotta take care of us," she said.

Her words of ignorance infuriated me more. "You must not be getting it. He is never going to be the same, never!" I yelled.

I punched the wall with all my strength. My adrenaline must have been high because I didn't feel the pain, or the blood coming from my right hand a couple of seconds later. My mother heard the noise and quickly came into the room. "What happened?" she asked.

I was angry that my dad didn't seem to think of the effect his alcoholism would have on our family.

"Nothing, I just can't stand my father!" I replied.

"Stop being stupid and come to the kitchen so I can clean it," my mother said in Spanish.

While cleaning my cut, my mother said, "I know you're mad, but if you should be mad at anyone, it's me. I chose him to be your father and couldn't see that he had a problem."

"No Ma, it's not your fault. It's his fault and his only. How could he call himself a man? What kind of a man has kids and just gives up? Because that's what he did with us," I said, walking away.

I was mad for a week until I realized I could not afford to sit around blaming my father, because it would get us nowhere. What I needed to do was get a job.

The day after my 16th birthday, I began looking for work after school. I dressed in an oxford shirt, slacks, and dress shoes to show my seriousness and I went into store after store, asking for a job. But no one seemed interested after I told them my age.

That made me even more mad at my father. If it weren't for

him I wouldn't be in this position in the first place. I was legally old enough to have a job, but too young to spark interest from hiring managers. I was constantly stressed because all I saw were bills and my mother's worry. It was one of the worst feelings in the world, knowing what I had to do but not being able to because of a number. I felt like a prisoner of my age.

My father moved back in with us last summer. He had nowhere else to go and needed help to do daily tasks. So now we have one more person taking up space in the house. He can no longer drink because he takes medication that can't be mixed with alcohol. We still don't really communicate, so I'm not sure how he feels.

Sometimes I can see his frustration when he can't do something on his own. But I can't tell what's making him more upset: that he can't work and provide for us, or that he can't drink anymore.

It's not easy dealing with a loss like this. My sense of security and being taken care of is gone. I can no longer look at the man I once called Daddy, and I don't think I can ever forgive him. Maybe when I'm an adult I'll understand, but right now I can't.

The author was in high school when he wrote this story.

Nelle McKay

A Parent's Road to Recovery

By Rosita Pagan

When my daughter Noelle was 5 years old, she told me that her father was sexually molesting her when she went on weekend visits. As soon as she told me, I took Noelle to the hospital, got the court to terminate visits between my daughter and her father, and put Noelle in therapy.

But Noelle seemed to get worse, not better. She began touching herself and acting out of control. I felt helpless because nothing I did seemed to put her at ease.

I did everything I could think of to handle my stress: family therapy, stress management classes, meditation, acupuncture, massages. But none of it helped me feel better.

I tried to talk to my husband and my sister about how depressed and overwhelmed I felt. My husband would tell me, "I'm here for you." My sister would say, "Don't worry, you'll be all right." Their comments would only make me more upset. I would say to myself, "What is wrong with these people? Don't they understand what I'm going through?"

I had an intense feeling of worthlessness. I believed I should have been able to protect my daughter. My children meant the world to me and I put everything else second, but it seemed like all my caring and hopes just didn't matter.

One night when I was angry, I decided to drink one beer, then another, then another. For the first time in months, I could feel the ease inside me. I felt calm.

After that, I began drinking more and more often, until I was having a beer first thing in the morning. I saw myself as a helpless mother and I saw my family as so messed up that whatever I did wouldn't make a difference. I honestly felt that if I went away and never returned, I wouldn't be missed.

I got to the point where I couldn't function without having a beer first. If I woke up in the morning and there wasn't any or someone threw out the one I had left, I would catch a fit. No matter what time it was, I was going outside to find a 24-hour store so I could get a beer.

My youngest daughter, Maya, was only 7 months old. One day I took her out for a stroll and I got an alcohol-related seizure. I fell and hit the edge of the sidewalk, and Maya fell, too. I ended up in the hospital for four days. When I saw the damage I'd done to myself, I started to cry. I was so scared. I decided to stop drinking cold turkey.

But that made me feel sick from withdrawal, so I continued drinking. I had a theory that if I wanted to stay safe, I could drink just a little. That was dumb, but in my way of "stinking thinking," it made sense.

Finally, after about a year, Noelle's therapist called the Administration for Children's Services (ACS) to report that I came to appointments smelling like a brewery, and they came knocking on my door.

When ACS first came I didn't think anything bad would happen. Despite my drinking, I saw my home as being in order. The children were healthy and well-fed. I wondered, "Why are they here?"

On the first visit I was sober and the caseworker said he would come a couple of times, then close the case. He asked me some basic questions about my children and left.

On the second visit, I had already had a couple of beers.

On the third visit there was a glass of beer on the table, and I'd just had a huge argument with my husband. I was extremely upset, because for the first time he called me names. What hurt me the most was when he said that I was an unfit mother and a "ho."

After that visit, my children went into care, and I went home to an empty apartment. I felt empty myself and went out to get drunk. I just didn't want to hurt anymore. Over the next few months, I felt kind of good only when I was drunk.

Because my children weren't home, I got less money from public assistance. I couldn't pay my rent, so I got evicted. I felt my life was over. I was homeless, childless, and shameless.

But that fall, ACS sent me to a substance abuse program called Women Connect. I felt like I didn't belong because I still did not believe I was an

I saw myself as a helpless mother and I saw my family as so messed up that whatever I did wouldn't make a difference.

alcoholic. I was in denial. For three months, I argued with the workers and didn't take the program and its rules seriously. But it turned out to be the beginning of a new life for me.

I was blessed with Ms. Torres, my substance abuse counselor. She decided she was going to show me tough love. She felt that outpatient rehab wasn't serious enough for me.

On day in January I went to the program like usual, and Ms. Torres was waiting for me. She told me to go back home and get some clothes. She said, "I've been watching you for three months. It's time to get better. You've hit rock bottom and it's time for you to get up."

She sent me to detox and then to a residential rehab program upstate. My experience in rehab was one that I will never forget.

I've never been in jail, but the way the rules in rehab were I felt like I was locked up. Every minute of the day was scheduled with groups and meals.

One day the director of the Spanish group asked me, "Do you love your children?"

I told him "Yes, I do, very much."

He replied "No, you don't." We went back and forth.

"How can you stand there and tell me I don't love my children?" I asked.

He said, "Because if you did love your children you wouldn't need our services."

I felt stunned, like someone hit me over the head with a rock. He was right. His comment made me feel I needed to get serious about my rehabilitation so I could love my girls like a real mother should.

During all of these meetings everyone would introduce themselves like, "I'm so-and-so and I'm an addict." But I didn't believe I was an alcoholic, so I would just say, "I'm Rosita."

In rehab I learned to love myself again and to feel strong despite feelings like shame, betrayal, and worthlessness.

But listening to all the other members of the group expressing their pain and turmoil, I got scared. I didn't want my alcoholism to escalate to something I couldn't get help for. Hearing other people talk about their addiction made me finally realize I had a problem. I knew my problem was serious, and that my girls were removed because of my actions.

One morning, after about three weeks, when it was my turn to introduce myself I said, "Good morning, my name is Rosita and I'm an alcoholic." To my surprise all of the other members of the group started clapping and saying, "She finally admitted it." That was a great feeling. I think that the group was just waiting for me to come to my senses.

In rehab I learned to love myself again and to feel strong

despite feelings like shame, betrayal, and worthlessness. I learned that, while drinking, I couldn't be of any use to anyone because my main concern was getting drunk. By staying sober, not only would I see things more clearly, but my feelings would be more intact. I also learned to appreciate and value different things in life. I started to understand that I should value all my time with my children, even when they get me upset.

After I graduated from the inpatient rehab, it was kind of difficult to go back to Women Connect. Facing Ms. Torres without my mask of anger was overwhelming. It was hard to let her know that she was right about me.

Ms. Torres looked at me and said, "I knew there was a good person under all that drinking." I was determined to stay sober and get my life back together.

I started attending a group called "Coping and Connecting." In the group, women would say how they felt at that moment, and we'd talk about ways to cope with those feelings. This group was intended to help parents who had or have an addiction problem cope with their sobriety. It also helps you understand that there are going to be a lot of conflicts and ups and downs during your journey to becoming a family again.

These groups helped me understand that not only did I need help, but my children needed help understanding that things were going to be different. While I was under the influence, setting rules and regulations wasn't my thing. Now that I was sober, I'd have to set some.

At first my children thought, "I don't have to follow these rules." It helped to explain to them that these rules were not to punish them but to help them become better people.

It took a long time after I completed rehab for my children to come home. That first day the girls were so happy. At first they didn't believe they were really coming home, because I picked them up like it was a regular weekend visit. But I told them, "Say goodbye to Sandra. This day is the last day you'll live with

Sandra."

"Why?" asked Noelle.

"Because you and Maya are home for good." The girls were cheering. I could see in their eyes the joy they felt.

It's been almost three years now since the girls came home. It feels good to be a mom again. Things are better, especially because I found Noelle an excellent therapist who is helping her deal with the sexual abuse. The past is always going to be a part of our lives, and I hope what happened is a lesson well-learned for all of us. But I feel like we're not dwelling on the hurt.

While I was under the influence, setting rules and regulations wasn't my thing. Now that I was sober, I'd have to set some.

Today Noelle, Maya, and I have a better mother-daughters relationship. We take the time to talk about each problem and try to come up with a solution or understanding.

My girls and I have special time together. My favorite time is when we watch TV together, literally connected. I lay on the sofa, Noelle lays on my legs, and Maya lays beside me. We've made a pact to do this at least once a week.

Rosita Pagan is a writer for Rise, *a magazine by and for parents involved in the child welfare system.*
www.risemagazine.org

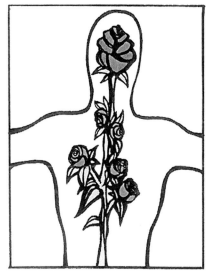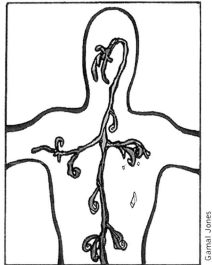

Gamal Jones

Does Rehab Work?
Explaining drug treatment

By Joe Ballew

When I was put in care because my parents had a substance abuse problem, I heard about something called rehab. I learned that was short for "rehabilitation," which means "to restore to good condition." But I wanted to know how rehab works, and whether it really helps parents stop drinking and doing drugs so we can go back home to them.

To better understand rehab, I interviewed two experts: Dr. Kim Sumner-Mayer, a family therapist, and Raye Barbieri, a social worker. Both of them have experience working with children and adults from addicted families.

Sumner-Mayer told me that rehab can definitely help people who have serious problems with substance abuse, but it may not work on everyone the first time.

There are several different types of rehab. **Inpatient treatment** requires people to live in treatment facilities for up to two years. Sometimes these patients first go through a 28-day program called **short-term detox**, to help them get the drugs out of their system.

Some patients only go to short-term detox. But research shows that inpatient treatment of at least six months works best for people who are severely addicted. With longer-term inpatient care, patients can learn how to stay sober.

Phoenix House, the drug treatment organization where Sumner-Mayer works, runs several inpatient centers in New York. Clients there wake up at 6 a.m., do chores, go to meetings and have classes about how to handle stress and cope with the feelings that make them want to use drugs and alcohol. They may also visit with family members and work on getting jobs and educations.

Whether or not your parent is able to recover, you should figure out how to get help for yourself.

People aren't forced to stay (there are no locks on the doors), but if a judge orders someone to complete rehab and he doesn't, he can wind up in jail. Rehab can be hard to complete because there are a lot of rules, and lots of drug addicts and alcoholics are not used to following rules.

About 60% of all people who go to rehab use **outpatient treatment**. That means the person lives at home but goes to a program almost every day to take rehab classes and get counseling. They spend up to 20 hours a week at this place.

Another kind of rehab is **self-help** offered by groups such as Alcoholics Anonymous and Narcotics Anonymous. After people leave inpatient or outpatient treatment, they may continue going to self-help groups to help them stay sober.

No professionals supervise self-help groups, and the only cost is a donation. People come to these groups to help themselves and each other by sharing advice, experience, and stories so they can stay motivated to keep sober.

Sometimes people have a **relapse**. That means they go back to using drugs or alcohol. Slightly more than half of all people who go through rehab have a relapse within two years of completing treatment. And 44% wind up getting treatment again within three years of going to rehab.

That doesn't mean they will never recover. Motivation is a major factor, but sometimes treatment can work even if a person isn't eager to quit. "Lots of people go to rehab because they don't want to go to jail, but many of them still end up having a successful treatment," said Sumner-Mayer.

Why doesn't rehab work on everyone? "It can be difficult for people who are drinking or using drugs to think clearly about what they need to do," Barbieri explained.

Also, giving up an addiction can be really difficult. You may feel sick for a while before you feel better, Sumner-Mayer told me.

Whether or not your parent is able to recover, you should figure out how to get help for yourself. Support groups like Alateen give children of alcoholics or drug users a place to talk about how they were affected by their parents' addiction. And Sumner-Mayer said we must always remember The Three C's: "You didn't Cause your parent's addiction, you can't Control your parent's addiction, and you can't Cure your parent's addiction."

Joe was 15 when he wrote this story.

Terrence Taylor

Leaving Her Behind

By Tamara

My hands began to tremble as I reached for the telephone, know-ing it was time to reveal to my mother the troubles that had been on my mind for quite some time now. 1-7-1-8... For each number I dialed, my heart skipped 10 beats. Then the phone began to ring.

All the thoughts in my head were tangled like a rope. "Should I say hello Mother, or hello Mommy? Should I just get straight to the point? Maybe I should just hang up now."

After a few rings, she finally picked up.

"Hello?"

My words were caught in my throat and it didn't seem like they'd be coming out anytime soon.

"Ummm, Mommy?"

"Yes?" she said.

"It's Tamara, and I have something to tell you." My voice had already begun to wither away.

"What's the matter, what is it?" she asked with concern in her voice.

"I don't want to come back home, and neither does Tanya. It's not that we don't love you, it's just that we'd feel better if we stayed with Tasha. Please don't be mad."

There was a brief silence. Then my mother spoke.

"No, it's OK, I understand. I know that I can't provide you guys with everything you need right now, and Tasha is just doing a better job than I can. Trust me, I'm not upset. It's fine."

"OK," I said, feeling somewhat relieved. We exchanged I love you's and hung up, but afterward I kept replaying the conversation in my head, thinking: If everything is fine, then why do I feel so bad?

Telling my mother I wasn't planning on coming back home to her was one of the hardest things I've ever done. I'd recently moved in with my 22-year-old sister, Tasha, because my mother had started using drugs. It wasn't the first time.

When I was 2, my brothers and sisters and I were placed in foster care because of her drug use. She got clean and regained custody of us four years later. I remember being so excited about going home. All I wanted was to be with my mother.

For the past 10 years I'd been trying not to think the worst about my mother, but I couldn't ignore what was right in front of me.

After we moved back home, my mom stayed clean for 10 years. But that didn't mean things were good. My mother was always yelling, making mountains out of molehills. She cursed at me every day, saying things so cruel that sometimes I hated ever having been born.

I tuned her out most of the time. I didn't want to believe that those words were coming from my mother's mouth. Other times I thought that by yelling back or ignoring her I could get across that I was tired of being disrespected and never being heard. But that didn't work.

Still, she was my mother, and we had our good days. If I was feeling sad, she would say things to make me feel better. Sometimes we would just sit and talk about any and everything that was on our minds (although if I told her something in confidence she'd sometimes use it against me later). Our relationship was a roller coaster. But I'd been on the ride for so long that getting off wasn't even an option.

Then, last summer, things escalated. I'd started seeing drastic changes in my mother, physically and emotionally. She was going from job to job, she was losing a lot of weight, there was never any food, and the arguments we had became way more intense, and more violent. Once she slammed my head against a mirror, angry that I'd told Tasha how she'd blown the money meant to pay for our brother's 8th grade graduation.

All these things were major clues to my mother's drug addiction, but I didn't want to believe she was at it again. I kept hoping things would get better, until one huge incident put the icing on the cake.

It was my birthday, and Tasha had just given me $100 as a present. My special day was going perfectly. I went to the movies with my sister, and all my friends had shown major love.

As I was getting ready to go to bed, my mother came up to me with a childish innocence to her voice, asking how much money Tasha had given me. Instantly I felt my temperature rising. "I know she is not about to ask me what I think she's about to ask me!" I thought.

"$100, why?"

"$100? Wow, that's a lot of money!"

"Yes, I guess so," I said with apathy in my voice.

"So can I ask you for a favor?"

"What do you want?" I replied warily.

"Can I borrow some money so I can buy a Metrocard to go to work tomorrow?"

I was outraged. "I can't believe she even has the audacity to ask me for money," I thought. "She hasn't even been to work in like 50 million years." I was so angry I blurted out my thoughts. My mom gave me a look of disappointment.

"Wow, Mara, so it's like that?" she said. "But I'm your mother. Please?" She repeated her plea again and again, until I finally gave in and handed her $10.

When I woke up the next morning, a voice in my head kept urging me to check my purse where I'd left the rest of my $100. I looked inside. Only $8 remained. A wave of panic came over me. "What the hell? Where's my money?" I woke up Tanya, my other sister, and told her what I'd discovered. For a short second our eyes connected, and I could tell she was thinking exactly what I was feeling.

"I think Mommy took it," she said, without hesitation. I wanted to give my mother the benefit of the doubt. But when we couldn't find the money anywhere, Tanya and I went to confront her.

"Mom…" I began to say, but Tanya immediately cut me off.

"Mara's money is missing, do you know where it is?"

"What?!" my mother yelled, as if she felt disrespected. "Do you think I took it?"

"Yes," my sister and I said simultaneously.

"Well, did you?" I asked. At this point it felt as though my body was there, but my mind was frozen solid, making it harder for me to say all the things I wanted to.

She kept denying it, but she wouldn't look me in my eyes, not even once. She had liar written all over her face. I wasn't even angry, just disgusted that she could lower herself to such a level. And that's when I realized I'd been blind. For the past 10 years I'd been trying not to think the worst about my mother, but I couldn't ignore what I was seeing right in front of me. My heart sank.

Tanya and I decided to go stay with our oldest sister Tasha, who'd moved out of mom's house about 6 months earlier. Tasha's house was the one place where we knew we'd be welcomed at any time. I didn't think then about how long I wanted to stay. I just knew I had to get out of my mother's house fast.

You guys have to sleep in the living room, because I don't have enough space, OK?" Tasha said, after we told her what happened.

I looked around the cozy, half-lit room with eggshell-colored walls. The living room was bare because my sister had just recently moved in; there was nothing but the floor and the fancy curtains she'd bought to "spruce up the place." It was different, but I liked it.

"This is fine," I said calmly.

That night, while I lay on my "bed," (a bunch of quilts on top of quilts) I couldn't get to sleep. I tossed and turned, listening to the quiet. I thought to myself, "It's so quiet. No Mommy arguing with her girlfriend, no Mommy yelling at Tanya, no nothing. It's too quiet."

That's when it hit me: I had become so used to the fighting and screaming that I had become "addicted," in a sense. I needed to hear all the chaos just to get to sleep!

"I have been in the middle of all this commotion entirely too long," I thought. "If it has gotten this bad, maybe I shouldn't go home." This was my mother's second time using drugs, I reasoned. So even if she got clean, who was to say she'd stay clean? And even if she did, would we still argue as much as we used to? Would I be able to fully forgive her?

A few days later, Tasha ran into our mother on the street. She told us our mother had on some sneakers that were falling apart, her hair was ragged, and her skin looked bad. She hadn't been trying to get herself together as I'd hoped; in fact, she was looking worse than ever.

I remember the look on Tasha's face as she said this. It wasn't hurt, sadness, or even anger. She just looked discouraged. I took that day as a sign. To me it truly proved that my mother wasn't ready to be a fit parent again.

I imagined going home, waiting for my mother to get herself together. What if she couldn't? What if staying with her began interfering with my own life plans? In three years I was going to be 18, and probably already in college. If I went into foster care again, my world would go topsy-turvy again. That would certainly affect my schoolwork, and maybe even my mental health.

I didn't want to hurt my mother, but I felt like staying with Tasha long-term was the only way for me to be in control of all aspects of my life.

For the next couple of days, all I could think was "I don't want to go home, I don't want to go home." But I had to figure out how to tell Tasha. Would she let me stay? Before I took that huge risk, I talked to Tanya. She told me she didn't want to go home, either.

When we told Tasha how we felt, her only response was, "Well, if you don't want to go home, then I'm not going to make you."

A couple of days later, we all went to the social services office so that we would legally be able to stay with Tasha while she tried to get temporary custody. From there we had a month of court dates, only two of which my mother showed up for. Both times, my mother was enraged, and it was almost impossible to talk to her.

After a couple of weeks, we started having supervised visits with her at the agency. My mother was like another person during these visits. She'd talk about how she couldn't wait for us to come home, and how everything was going to be different. I didn't believe her anymore, and I didn't want to let her continue this wishful thinking. I knew I had to tell her soon, but I just couldn't do it face to face. That's why I called her.

After I'd hung up the phone with my mother, I just lay down feeling overwhelmed with worry. I should've been relieved, but I felt terrible, because I knew that in some way I was breaking my mother's heart. But I also I knew that staying with Tasha was the best thing for me.

It's been about two months now since I made that call to my mother, and our relationship has become a love-hate type of thing. Sometimes we still laugh together, but most of the time we just can't stand to be around one another. There's a lot of screaming and yelling, and sometimes we both say things we don't mean, like "I hate you," or "You're the worst person in the world." We apologize later, but I feel like she's punishing me for refusing to live with her.

Now that Tanya and I are living permanently with Tasha, my mother is always making smart remarks that get me upset. She says things like, "This is all about me and Travis (my brother) now," since Travis is the only child living with her now.

My mom would talk about how she couldn't wait for us to come home, and how everything was going to be different. I didn't believe her anymore.

She even gave Travis our old room, and when we asked her why, she replied, "Why do you two care anyway, you guys aren't even coming home." When she said that, I felt like she didn't care about me anymore and that hurt. It was like she was cutting me out of her life, and so I started to do the same.

Living with Tasha is still great. Of course there are times when she makes me angry, and we have our disagreements, but that's part of every sibling relationship. I've had to make some adjustments, too, because she's not only my sister but my legal guardian. That means I have to listen to the things she tells me. It gets annoying sometimes, but it's worth it.

Unlike living with my mom, Tasha actually takes the time to listen to me, treats me with respect, and values my opinion. She is the only person I completely trust. She makes me feel safe and wanted.

Recently I've been thinking a lot about how my relationship with my mother has affected my relationships with other people in my life. It's hard for me to trust even my closest friends. Even trying to tell someone that I love them is hard for me. I've barricaded myself against the hurt, pain, and disappointment, but this isn't the kind of person I want to continue to be.

Right now, I can't really see myself making amends with my mother. I'm at a point in my life where I am learning how to get rid of the people I don't really need, and how to cherish the ones I do.

I used to think that because someone is family you need them in your life, but now I see that that isn't always the case. At times, family can hurt you the most. Sometimes, when the negativity becomes so monotonous, you just have to learn how to walk away.

Tamara was 16 when she wrote this story.

YC Art Dept.

Something You Can't Fix

Naomi Weinstein, director of the Center on Addiction and the Family in New York City, explains what you should know if your parent has a substance abuse problem.

Q: When is a parent's alcohol or drug use a problem?

A: If the parent's use is causing problems in your life, that's a problem. If you have to lie for your parent, or cover for them, or get them ready for work, or they're embarrassing you by showing up drunk or high, that's a problem. It doesn't mean your parent doesn't love you. But it does mean the drug has hijacked your parent's brain. The drugs are in control.

Q: What do you do if your parent is using drugs, or if you think they're drinking too much?

A: If your parent has a substance abuse problem, that's not your fault and it's not something that you can fix. You need to focus on keeping yourself safe. Find a trusted adult who will give you a safe place to do your homework or get fed. That might be a neighbor, a relative, or someone like a teacher or school nurse.

You should also find someone who you can talk to, who can help you understand what's happening. Someone in your family, or another person in recovery, can help you understand addiction and what the facts are.

Q: If you tell someone, will they put you into foster care?

A: That depends a lot on what kind of drug it is and how much it's causing your parent to neglect or abuse you and other children in the home. Right now, in New York, the child welfare system is trying whenever possible not to remove kids. But that's not a guarantee, and other states may have other priorities.

> *If your parent has a substance abuse problem, that's not your fault and it's not something that you can fix.*

If you do get removed from your home, you should always try to think of a friend or family member who can take you in, and tell your social worker that you want to stay with that person.

Q: Are kids whose parents are addicted to drugs or alcohol more likely to be addicted themselves?

A: Unfortunately, yes. When a parent has a substance abuse problem, their child is three to four times more likely to become addicted to drugs or alcohol. It's important to recognize your own risk for addiction, and take that very seriously. But that doesn't mean you're destined to become an addict. Most children of addicts do *not* become addicts themselves. And you can do things to protect yourself.

When you're angry or upset, don't turn to drugs or alcohol to deal with it. Find someone to talk to, or find places and activities that make you feel good about yourself. Figure out what your strengths are and take advantage of them. And remember that you're not alone. Somewhere between 1 in every 8 to 1 in every 4 kids is dealing with an alcoholic parent. Among kids in foster care, 50-80% have a parent who is a substance abuser.

Q: How can you help yourself cope?

A: First of all, you should recognize that you need and deserve services, like mental health counseling and other kinds of support. You can contact Alateen (1-888-425-2666) to join a group of other teens who are dealing with an addiction in the family. Or talk to someone at school who you trust. If you're in the child welfare system, talk to your caseworker. Even if you think you're coping well, talking to someone can give you the support you need to become even stronger, and to cope with some pretty lousy things.

Be open to the kinds of support you do have, even when it comes from unexpected places.

Be open to the kinds of support you do have, even when it comes from unexpected places—while you want to have your mom's love and attention, it may be your grandma who provides it, or it may be your after-school teacher.

Q: If you reunify with a parent who has been to rehab, what can you expect?

A: It's going to be really tough. When families reunify, at first everyone is going to be on their best behavior. But after the honeymoon period is over, there's going to be a really turbulent stormy period, and an increase in fighting. It might actually feel like it's worse than it was before your parent got services.

Parents often report that their teen kids are so angry, and just curse them out, and the adults are bewildered because they just went though all this treatment. But the parent may have been gone or out of it for a long time, and suddenly they're trying to step back in and be mom or dad, and start imposing rules. And after so much time apart, and at a time when a teen is trying to

Something You Can't Fix

become an independent adult, trying to find that bond again is a very tough process for both parents and kids.

Plus, one thing mom or dad is going to learn in treatment is how to express their feelings, and that can lead to more conflict. Families often manage to stay together right through the addiction and then split up when they come home. That's why it's so important to get family therapy if at all possible.

Q: What can help families get through that reunification process?

A: Family therapy, time, and patience. Being able to know what's coming next can help. If something is predictable it's normal, and if it's normal it's not a tragedy. That stormy period takes everyone by surprise. Families think, "If things are this tough, something is wrong." But if they know that it's supposed to happen, then somehow it makes those things a little bit more tolerable, because it's normal.

It's very important for teens to know that when parents first get out the focus is on recovery. It takes four to five years before you really consider an alcoholic to be in a stable recovery place. Treatment is just the beginning of the recovery process. It requires a lot of patience.

Q: What can you do if you suspect your parent is using again?

A: Using drugs or alcohol again is the last stage of a process that starts with the person going back to their old values and attitudes and ways of behaving. If your parent was doing very well and always making their meetings, and then they start missing them, that's when you should say something.

Teens can ask another family member or close friend to step in and say, "I've noticed this happening, do you need to talk to somebody?" You can even call the treatment program and ask them to reach out directly. The idea is to prevent it from happening.

In a household where people are using illegal drugs there's

often a family culture not to tell anyone. There are families who do everything from completely denying what's happening, to putting the shades down so no one can see, to trying to behave really well so mom doesn't get stressed out and use. But none of those strategies work.

Addiction is a recurring disease and recovery isn't easy. The important thing to remember is that, as a teen, the best thing you can do is help yourself.

To find a support group near you, call Alateen/Al-Anon at 1-888-4AL-ANON (1-888-425-2666) or go to alateen.org.

Shattered

"Girl, where you at?"

Darcy Wills winced at the voice blasting through her new cell phone. It was her best friend, Tarah Carson, and she sounded angry.

"C'mon, Darce. You're late," Tarah scolded.

Darcy knew Tarah was right even before she looked at her watch. She should have left the house ten minutes ago. Instead she was staring at her reflection in the bathroom mirror, hoping Hakeem Randall wouldn't notice the guilt in her eyes or the worry that haunted her face. So much had changed in the few months since they'd broken up. *Too much*, Darcy thought.

"I'm sorry, Tarah. It's just that—"

"Tell her I'm starvin'," yelled Cooper Hodden, Tarah's boyfriend, in the background. "Tell her if she don't get here soon, I'ma start eatin' without her."

His voice was so loud Darcy held the cell phone away from

Here's the first chapter from *Shattered*, by Paul Langan, a novel about teens facing difficult situations like the ones you read about in this book. *Shattered* is one of several books in the Bluford Series™ by Townsend Press.

her ear. It sounded like he and Tarah were in the hallway, not several blocks away at Niko's Pizza.

"Stop talkin' nonsense, Coop," Tarah replied. "We ain't eatin' nothin' till she gets here."

"C'mon, Tar! Why you gotsta be that way?" Cooper complained. "Don't ya hear my stomach growlin'?"

"Hold on one second, girl," Tarah said.

Darcy listened as Tarah started hollering at Cooper. She put the phone down to inspect her face again, paying special attention to a tiny pimple just above her right eyebrow.

Why does it have to be there now, she thought, dabbing it with a bit of cover-up. She'd already covered it once, but she wanted to make sure it was invisible to Hakeem.

It wasn't the only thing she hoped to hide.

"Hello? You still there?" Tarah asked.

Darcy quickly grabbed the phone off the bathroom counter.

"Yeah, I'm leavin' right now," she replied. A jolt of nervous energy raced down her back, making her stomach tremble. An hour of trying on different outfits, messing with her hair, and putting on makeup hadn't calmed her nerves. She still felt tense about seeing Hakeem again, especially after what happened over the summer.

"You mean you didn't even leave yet?" Tarah shouted. Darcy held the phone away from her ear again, but there was no escaping her friend's yelling. "We was supposed to meet fifteen minutes ago!"

"I know. I'm sorry, but things were busy at Scoops, and my manager made me stay late," Darcy lied, annoyed at herself for being dishonest with her best friend.

It was true the ice cream store had a busy day. Though it was early September, the weather was as hot as mid-July, and Scoops had been crammed with people buying ice cream. But Darcy's manager, Tamika Ardis, never asked her to stay late. Instead, she sent Darcy home early after she argued with a customer. Darcy had been rushing to prepare two milkshakes when she heard someone call out to her.

"Where's the rest of my change?"

Darcy turned to face a large woman with a tight weave. Two kids huddled close to the woman's legs, holding sticky, half-eaten ice cream cones that dripped onto the floor. Darcy had served them just a few minutes earlier.

"I already gave it to you, ma'am," Darcy replied.

"You better check your register or learn to count or somethin' 'cause I gave you a $20 bill. You just shortchanged me $10," the woman snapped, her free hand resting on her hips.

Darcy took a deep breath. All summer, she'd dealt with customers who treated her and her coworker Haley like trash. Usually Darcy just smiled and ignored it when people were mean, but today she didn't have any patience.

"You don't need to be rude, ma'am," Darcy replied. The words had slipped out so fast Darcy was stunned. So was Haley, who at that moment dropped a small chocolate sundae onto her cash register.

"*Excuse me?*" the woman said, nudging aside the person who'd been at the head of the line. "Girl, you best check that register and yo' mouth and give me my change, or I'ma make a scene up in here."

"Ma'am, let me finish with this customer first, and I'll help you," Darcy replied, still holding the milkshakes in her hands.

"No, you're gonna help me *now*. I waited in line once. I ain't waitin' again."

Darcy felt her temper building. She couldn't tell the customer off; that would only get her fired. And she couldn't admit she was too stressed to focus on her work. That would only make the woman angrier. For several long seconds, Darcy didn't know what to say. Her mind had gone blank.

"It's okay, ma'am. I can help you," Tamika cut in just in time. "Let's check the register."

Darcy watched as her manager unlocked the cash drawer. She was sure she hadn't miscounted. In her months on the job, she had made plenty of mistakes, but never with money. At Scoops and at Bluford High where she was about to start her junior year, numbers were always something Darcy was good at.

But inside the cash drawer, Tamika found a $20 bill sitting in the $10 slot. Darcy knew instantly she had made a mistake, and the customer had been right. Darcy felt her cheeks burn with embarrassment.

"I'm so sorry, ma'am," Darcy said as Tamika handed over the money.

"Mmm hmm." The woman scowled and walked out with her children.

"What's wrong with you, Darcy? I've never seen you act that way, and I never want to see it again," Tamika warned as soon as the store emptied out. "I can't afford to upset customers. It's hard enough to stay in business around here as it is."

"I'm sorry. I just got a lot on my mind."

"I hope it's not serious, Darcy. I need you around here. I wish I had two of you."

"No, it's not. It's just . . ." Darcy paused, trying to decide how honest she should be. Tamika recently offered to increase her hours. Darcy didn't want her to change her mind.

"It's her boyfriend, I mean *ex-boyfriend*," cut in Haley, her blond ponytail poking through the back of her green Scoops visor.

Darcy's jaw dropped. Haley had promised never to tell anyone what they discussed at work, especially not Tamika.

"He's been in Detroit for months, and tonight she's gonna see him for the first time since he got back. She doesn't want to admit it, but she's really excited," Haley continued with a smile. "And kinda nervous too."

"*Haley, shut your mouth!*" Darcy snapped, embarrassed to hear her personal life being discussed with her boss. "That was between you and me."

"Relax, Darcy. I'm just telling her why you're so out of it. It's not like she hasn't noticed. You're on another planet today," Haley explained.

"I'm *not* out of it. I just miscounted some change, that's all. Not like you never made a mistake, Haley."

"Don't even go there, Darce. This isn't about me, and you know it."

Darcy knew Haley was right. All day, she kept forgetting customers' orders. It got so bad she started writing everything down like her first week on the job. Even when she tried to listen to people, all Darcy could hear were the questions racing through her mind.

Should I tell Hakeem about what happened to me this summer?

If I tell him the truth, will he blame me or think I'm a bad person? Will we ever get back together?

"Haley's right," Tamika said, putting a hand on Darcy's shoulder.

"But—"

"It's okay, Darcy. I know you're a great worker, but today you're having a bad day. Lord knows I've had my share. When I think about it, almost all of them have to do with men," Tamika said with a knowing smile. "Why don't you take the rest of the afternoon off. Haley and I can handle things until closing."

"Are you serious?" Darcy asked. It felt wrong to have everyone know her business, but she needed the break to clear her head and get ready.

"Yeah, go and have fun. Not too much fun, though," Tamika said.

"And whatever you do, be sure someone else counts your change tonight," Haley teased.

Darcy left Scoops in a daze. It was true Hakeem distracted her from work, but there were other things tugging at her too. The summer had been like the earthquakes that sometimes cracked sidewalks and shattered windows in her neighborhood. Only this time, the quake centered on Darcy's house. She still felt aftershocks.

Grandma's quiet death in the bedroom next to Darcy's.

Her parents' announcement that they were having a baby.

Her old friend Brisana's pregnancy scare.

Deeper still was what happened one afternoon just after she and Hakeem broke up. That's when Brian Mason came around with his shiny red Toyota, his smooth voice and wide, dark shoulders. He was nineteen. Darcy babysat for his sister, Liselle. Just thinking of Brian made Darcy nauseous.

Should I tell Hakeem what happened?

For a while, it seemed like a question she wouldn't have to answer. The day Hakeem left, Darcy was sure she'd never see him again. His father was battling cancer, and his family was broke from medical bills. Their only choice was to move in with relatives in faraway Detroit. Hakeem and Darcy split up just before they left.

The loss crushed Darcy. Her boyfriend for most of their sophomore year, Hakeem had also been one of her closest friends at Bluford. He had stood by her no matter what drama was happening in her life, and there had been plenty, especially since her father returned after abandoning the family for five years. When they said goodbye for the last time, they promised to stay in touch and to always be honest with each other.

Darcy hadn't kept that promise.

For months, she ignored the voice in her head, the one that made her feel guilty whenever she stared at Hakeem's picture collecting dust in her room.

Then a miracle happened. Hakeem's father's health improved, and he allowed his son to live with Cooper and return to Bluford High. Darcy was thrilled beyond words at the news, but her past with Brian still haunted her.

There was no way she could tell Hakeem what happened. No

way she could admit she'd gone to Brian's apartment to be alone with him. No way she could say Brian soothed the ache she felt when Hakeem left. And there was something else she couldn't confess to Hakeem.

Brian had gone too far. They had been on his couch kissing, and everything was okay until he tried to work his hands under her shirt.

"Relax," he said when she grabbed his hand.

Then she felt him tugging at her clothes again. His scratchy palm slid against the sensitive skin of her stomach. This time, she told him point-blank to stop. She even tried to push him away. He got angry.

"You're acting like a baby!" he yelled. She tried to get off the couch, but he was too strong. Within seconds, he had her pinned. Sometimes she could still feel how he held her down, his hands gripping her like chains, his strong body pressing against hers. For a frightening instant, she realized she couldn't escape him.

But her father arrived and stopped Brian in his tracks.

"If you ever mess with my daughter again, it will be the last mistake you make!" Dad yelled with a wild rage in his eyes, slamming Brian against a wall. Brian moved out a few days later, but the damage was done.

For weeks afterward, Darcy relived the attacks in nightmares. In them, Brian was even more violent, and Dad never arrived to save her. The dreams got so severe she couldn't sleep. Then she started having panic attacks. Things got so bad Darcy told her parents and Tarah about her problem. She even met for weeks with a counselor at the community center where Tarah worked. Over time, the nightmares and panic attacks faded. But the scars were still there.

Darcy felt them gnawing at her as she left Scoops. Felt them as she prepared to meet Hakeem for the first time since he returned. Felt them even now as she spoke with Tarah on her cell phone.

"Look, Darce, are you comin' out or not?" Tarah asked, shattering her thoughts.

Darcy sighed and put her makeup away.

"I'll be there, Tar'," she said. "Ten minutes. I promise."

"If you're not, we're comin' over there and draggin' you out," Tarah warned.

"I'll be there," Darcy repeated, smoothing out her shirt one last time and inspecting the way her body filled her jeans. "I'm leaving right now."

Tarah hung up, and Darcy headed out the door, rushing toward Niko's.

Should I tell Hakeem what happened?

She still didn't know the answer.

Shattered, *a Bluford Series™ novel, is reprinted with permission from Townsend Press. Copyright © 2002.*

If you'd like to continue reading this book, it is available for $1/copy from TownsendPress.com. Or tell an adult (like your teacher) that they can receive copies of *Shattered* for free if they order a class set of 15 or more copies of *Watching My Parents Disappear*. To order, call 212-279-0708 x115 or visit www.youthcomm.org.

Teens:
How to Get More Out of This Book

Self-help: The teens who wrote the stories in this book did so because they hope that telling their stories will help readers who are facing similar challenges. They want you to know that you are not alone, and that taking specific steps can help you manage or overcome very difficult situations. They've done their best to be clear about the actions that worked for them so you can see if they'll work for you.

Writing: You can also use the book to improve your writing skills. Each teen in this book wrote 5-10 drafts of his or her story before it was published. If you read the stories closely you'll see that the teens work to include a beginning, a middle, and an end, and good scenes, description, dialogue, and anecdotes (little stories). To improve your writing, take a look at how these writers construct their stories. Try some of their techniques in your own writing.

Reading: Finally, you'll notice that we include the first chapter from a Bluford Series novel in this book, alongside the true stories by teens. We hope you'll like it enough to continue reading. The more you read, the more you'll strengthen your reading skills. Teens at Youth Communication like the Bluford novels because they explore themes similar to those in their own stories. Your school may already have the Bluford books. If not, you can order them online for only $1.

Resources on the Web

We will occasionally post Think About It questions on our website, www.youthcomm.org, to accompany stories in this and other Youth Communication books. We try out the questions with teens and post the ones they like best. Many teens report that writing answers to those questions in a journal is very helpful.

How to Use This Book in Staff Training

Staff say that reading these stories gives them greater insight into what teens are thinking and feeling, and new strategies for working with them. You can help the staff you work with by using these stories as case studies.

Select one story to read in the group, and ask staff to identify and discuss the main issue facing the teen. There may be disagreement about this, based on the background and experience of staff. That is fine. One point of the exercise is that teens have complex lives and needs. Adults can probably be more effective if they don't focus too narrowly and can see several dimensions of their clients.

Ask staff: What issues or feelings does the story provoke in them? What kind of help do they think the teen wants? What interventions are likely to be most promising? Least effective? Why? How would you build trust with the teen writer? How have other adults failed the teen, and how might that affect his or her willingness to accept help? What other resources would be helpful to this teen, such as peer support, a mentor, counseling, family therapy, etc?

Resources on the Web

From time to time we will post Think About It questions on our website, www.youthcomm.org, to accompany stories in this and other Youth Communication books. We try out the questions with teens and post the ones that they find most effective. We'll also post lessons for some of the stories. Adults can use the questions and lessons in workshops.

Teachers and Staff:
How to Use This Book in Groups

When working with teens individually or in groups, you can use these stories to help young people face difficult issues in a way that feels safe to them. That's because talking about the issues in the stories usually feels safer to teens than talking about those same issues in their own lives. Addressing issues through the stories allows for some personal distance; they hit close to home, but not too close. Talking about them opens up a safe place for reflection. As teens gain confidence talking about the issues in the stories, they usually become more comfortable talking about those issues in their own lives.

Below are general questions to guide your discussion. In most cases you can read a story and conduct a discussion in one 45-minute session. Teens are usually happy to read the stories aloud, with each teen reading a paragraph or two. (Allow teens to pass if they don't want to read.) It takes 10-15 minutes to read a story straight through. However, it is often more effective to let workshop participants make comments and discuss the story as you go along. The workshop leader may even want to annotate her copy of the story beforehand with key questions.

If teens read the story ahead of time or silently, it's good to break the ice with a few questions that get everyone on the same page: Who is the main character? How old is she? What happened to her? How did she respond? Another good starting question is: "What stood out for you in the story?" Go around the room and let each person briefly mention one thing.

Then move on to open-ended questions, which encourage participants to think more deeply about what the writers were feeling, the choices they faced, and the actions they took. There are no right or wrong answers to the open-ended questions.

Open-ended questions encourage participants to think about how the themes, emotions, and choices in the stories relate to their own lives. Here are some examples of open-ended questions that we have found to be effective. You can use variations of these questions with almost any story in this book.

—What main problem or challenge did the writer face?

—What choices did the teen have in trying to deal with the problem?

—Which way of dealing with the problem was most effective for the teen? Why?

—What strengths, skills, or resources did the teen use to address the challenge?

—If you were in the writer's shoes, what would you have done?

—What could adults have done better to help this young person?

—What have you learned by reading this story that you didn't know before?

—What, if anything, will you do differently after reading this story?

—What surprised you in this story?

—Do you have a different view of this issue, or see a different way of dealing with it, after reading this story? Why or why not?

Credits

The stories in this book originally appeared in the following Youth Communication publications:

"House of Cards," by Chaquana Townsend, *Represent*, September/October 2007; "'I Think These Drugs Are Daddy's,'" by Anonymous, *Represent*, September/October 2007; "The Man in the Glass," by Jessica F., *New Youth Connections*, March 2005; "Watching My Parents Disappear," by T.M., *Represent*, March/April 2004; "Parent to Your Parents?," by T.M., *Represent*, March/April 2004; "Making It on My Own," by D.B., *Represent*, September/October 2007; "A Second Chance," by Karen Haynesworth, *Represent*, November/December 2002; "I Bounced," by Anonymous, *New Youth Connections*, December 1999; "Doing Time in the Hood," by Lakia Holmes, *Represent*, September/October 2001; "Starting Over Without Them," by Hattie Rice, *Represent*, March/April 2004; "Man of the House," by Anonymous, *New Youth Connections*, November 2003; "A Parent's Road to Recovery," by Rosita Pagan, *Represent*, September/October 2007; "Does Rehab Work?: Explaining Drug Treatment," by Joe Ballew, *Represent*, September/October 2007; "Leaving Her Behind," by Tamara, *Represent*, March/April 2008; "Something You Can't Fix," *Represent*, September/October 2007.

About
Youth Communication

Youth Communication, founded in 1980, is a nonprofit youth development program located in New York City whose mission is to teach writing, journalism, and leadership skills. The teenagers we train become writers for our websites and books and for two print magazines: *New Youth Connections*, a general-interest youth magazine, and *Represent*, a magazine by and for young people in foster care.

Each year, up to 100 young people participate in Youth Communication's school-year and summer journalism workshops, where they work under the direction of full-time professional editors. Most are African-American, Latino, or Asian, and many are recent immigrants. The opportunity to reach their peers with accurate portrayals of their lives and important self-help information motivates the young writers to create powerful stories.

Our goal is to run a strong youth development program in which teens produce high quality stories that inform and inspire their peers. Doing so requires us to be sensitive to the complicated lives and emotions of the teen participants while also providing an intellectually rigorous experience. We achieve that goal in the writing/teaching/editing relationship, which is the core of our program.

Our teaching and editorial process begins with discussions

between adult editors and the teen staff. In those meetings, the teens and the editors work together to identify the most important issues in the teens' lives and to figure out how those issues can be turned into stories that will resonate with teen readers.

Once story topics are chosen, students begin the process of crafting their stories. For a personal story, that means revisiting events in one's past to understand their significance for the future. For a commentary, it means developing a logical and persuasive point of view. For a reported story, it means gathering information through research and interviews. Students look inward and outward as they try to make sense of their experiences and the world around them and find the points of intersection between personal and social concerns. That process can take a few weeks or a few months. Stories frequently go through ten or more drafts as students work under the guidance of their editors, the way any professional writer does.

Many of the students who walk through our doors have uneven skills, as a result of poor education, living under extremely stressful conditions, or coming from homes where English is a second language. Yet, to complete their stories, students must successfully perform a wide range of activities, including writing and rewriting, reading, discussion, reflection, research, interviewing, and typing. They must work as members of a team and they must accept individual responsibility. They learn to provide constructive criticism, and to accept it. They engage in explorations of truthfulness, fairness, and accuracy. They meet deadlines. They must develop the audacity to believe that they have something important to say and the humility to recognize that saying it well is not a process of instant gratification. Rather, it usually requires a long, hard struggle through many discussions and much rewriting.

It would be impossible to teach these skills and dispositions as separate, disconnected topics, like grammar, ethics, or assertiveness. However, we find that students make rapid progress when they are learning skills in the context of an inquiry that is personally significant to them and that will benefit their peers.

When teens publish their stories—in *New Youth Connections* and *Represent*, on the Web, and in other publications—they reach tens of thousands of teen and adult readers. Teachers, counselors, social workers, and other adults circulate the stories to young people in their classes and out-of-school youth programs. Adults tell us that teens in their programs—including many who are ordinarily resistant to reading—clamor for the stories. Teen readers report that the stories give them information they can't get anywhere else, and inspire them to reflect on their lives and open lines of communication with adults.

Writers usually participate in our program for one semester, though some stay much longer. Years later, many of them report that working here was a turning point in their lives—that it helped them acquire the confidence and skills that they needed for success in college and careers. Scores of our graduates have overcome tremendous obstacles to become journalists, writers, and novelists. They include National Book Award finalist and MacArthur Fellowship winner Edwidge Danticat, novelist Ernesto Quiñonez, writer Veronica Chambers, and *New York Times* reporter Rachel Swarns. Hundreds more are working in law, business, and other careers. Many are teachers, principals, and youth workers, and several have started nonprofit youth programs themselves and work as mentors—helping another generation of young people develop their skills and find their voices.

Youth Communication is a nonprofit educational corporation. Contributions are gratefully accepted and are tax deductible to the fullest extent of the law.

To make a contribution, or for information about our publications and programs, including our catalog of over 100 books and curricula for hard-to-reach teens, see www.youthcomm.org

About The Editors

Laura Longhine is the editorial director at Youth Communication, where she oversees editorial work on the organization's books, websites, and magazines. She edited *Represent*, Youth Communication's magazine by and for teens in foster care, for three years.

Prior to joining Youth Communication, Longhine was as a staff writer at the *Free Times*, an alt-weekly in South Carolina, and a freelance reporter for various publications. Her stories have been published in *The New York Times*, *Legal Affairs*, newyorkmetro.com, and *Child Welfare Watch*. She has a bachelor's in English from Tufts University and a master's in journalism from Columbia University.

Longhine is the editor of several other Youth Communication books, including *The Fury Inside: Teens Write About Anger* and *Finding A Way Out: Teens Write About Surviving Relationship Abuse*.

Keith Hefner co-founded Youth Communication in 1980 and has directed it ever since. He is the recipient of the Luther P. Jackson Education Award from the New York Association of Black Journalists and a MacArthur Fellowship. He was also a Revson Fellow at Columbia University.

More Helpful Books
From Youth Communication

Do You Have What It Takes? A Comprehensive Guide to Success After Foster Care. In this survival manual, current and former foster teens show how they prepared not only for the practical challenges they've faced on the road to independence, but also the emotional ones. Worksheets and exercises help foster teens plan for their future. Activity pages at the end of each chapter help social workers, independent living instructors, and other leaders use the stories with individuals or in groups. (Youth Communication)

The Struggle to Be Strong: True Stories by Teens About Overcoming Tough Times. Foreword by Veronica Chambers. Help young people identify and build on their own strengths with 30 personal stories about resiliency. (Free Spirit)

Depression, Anger, Sadness: Teens Write About Facing Difficult Emotions. Give teens the confidence they need to seek help when they need it. These teens write candidly about difficult emotional problems—such as depression, cutting, and domestic violence—and how they have tried to help themselves. (Youth Communication)

What Staff Need to Know: Teens Write About What Works. How can foster parents, group home staff, caseworkers, social workers, and teachers best help teens? These stories show how communication can be improved on both sides, and provide insight into what kinds of approaches and styles work best. (Youth Communication)

Haunted By My Past: Teens Write About Surviving Sexual Abuse. Help teens feel less alone and more hopeful about overcoming the trauma of sexual abuse. This collection includes first-person accounts by male and female survivors grappling with fear, shame, and guilt. (Youth Communication)

 *Just the Two of Us: Teens Write About Building Good Relationships.* Show teens how to make and maintain healthy relationships (and avoid bad ones). Many teens in care have had poor role models and are emotionally vulnerable. These stories demonstrate good and bad choices teens make in friendship and romance. (Youth Communication)

The Fury Inside: Teens Write About Anger. Help teens manage their anger. These writers show how they got better control of their emotions and sought the support of others. (Youth Communication)

 *Always on the Move: Teens Write About Changing Homes and Staff.* Help teens feel less alone with these stories about how their peers have coped with the painful experience of frequent placement changes and turnover among staff and social workers. (Youth Communication)

Two Moms in My Heart: Teens Write About the Adoption Option. Teens will appreciate these stories by peers who describe how complicated the adoption experience can be—even when it should give them a more stable home than foster care. (Youth Communication)

 My Secret Addiction: Teens Write About Cutting. These true accounts of cutting, or self-mutilation, offer a window into the personal and family situations that lead to this secret habit, and show how teens can get the help they need. (Youth Communication)

The High That Couldn't Last: Teens and Drugs, From Experimentation to Addiction. Text to go here. These stories show why teens try drugs and the damage that can result. Real teens write about how they got hooked, what happened, and how they've struggled to get themselves back on track.. (Youth Communication)

To order these and other books, go to:
www.youthcomm.org
or call 212-279-0708 x115